THE IRON TRIANGLE

*Inside the Liberal Democrat Plan to use
Race to Divide Christians and Americans
in their Quest for Power and how
We can Defeat Them*

Vince Everett Ellison

outskirts
press

Questions Answered in _The Iron Triangle_:

Why have Christian Black Americans forsaken their God and their children to vote more than 90% for the Atheist/Anti-Christian Democrat Party?

Who is part of the Iron Triangle, and why is it so dangerous?

Why do White Christian Conservatives have nothing more for which to apologize?

How is the Democrat Party the longest unholy criminal enterprise in history?

Why is the act of African Americans freeing themselves from the Democrat Party essential for their survival…and for _American_ survival?

Why would the reconciliation of Black and White Christians save America and cause the destruction of the Iron Triangle and the Democrat Party?

Why is the sowing of racial discord, fear and hatred necessary for Democrats to maintain power?

How do Conservatives and Christians talk to and reconcile with their fellow Christians and countrymen who have been bombarded with a lifetime of lies from the Iron Triangle and the Democrat Party? Why would an intervention help?

Why will doing nothing result in the destruction of America and usher in era that will again cover the world in darkness?

This book is dedicated to my four teachers:

My Parents: Ivory Ellison and Ella Ellison
&
My In-Laws: Dr. John C. Calhoun and Chorsie Calhoun

TABLE OF CONTENTS

Prologue   i
Overview   v
Section 1: Vince Everett Ellison's Motivation   1
Section 2: Developing My Ideology   12
    The Con Game Exposed   12
    Poverty and Race Are Not the Problem   14
    Arguing with Icons   19
    Stockholm Syndrome & Cognitive Dissonance   21
    Cognitive Dissonance   37
    What Do We Believe?   41
Section 3: Three Sides of the Triangle   56
    The Black Preacher   56
    Souls to the Polls   69
    Communism, Marxism Infiltrate the "Black" Church   82
    By Their Fruits You Will Know Them   94
    The Second Side of the Triangle: The Politician   102
    The Democrat Death Cult   105
    The Party of Slavery, Secession, Segregation, Socialism
    and Slaughter   117
    The Daniel Test   139
    Third Side of the Triangle: Black Civic Organizations   141
    Sellout 1965   146
Section 4: Conclusion   162
    Liberals Are Dividing the Christians   166
    The Walk of Illumination   172
About the Author   173

PROLOGUE

"THESE NEGROES, THEY'RE getting pretty uppity these days . . . Now we've got to do something about this; we've got to give them a little something, just enough to quiet them down, not enough to make a difference . . . I'll have them niggers voting Democrat for the next two hundred years." Lyndon Baines Johnson, president of the United States of America, a Southern Democrat from the former Confederate state of Texas, was reported to have said this by LBJ biographer Doris Kearns Goodwin and Robert McMillan, steward on Air Force 1, in response to a question posed to him by a group of Southern Democrat governors regarding his support for the 1964 Civil Rights Act. History has painted Johnson as a champion of Black Americans, but this statement suggests he and the Democrats had a different motivation. On April 16, 2019 when speaking about congressional districts with large minority populations Speaker Of The House Nancy Pelosi triumphantly stated,while sipping a glass of water "This glass of water would win with a D next to its name in those districts". To say this so arrogantly without any fear a reprecusssions, is clear evidence that the Democrats believe they have control of, what Lyndon Johnson described as "them Niggers."

In the movie "*The Matrix*" when Morpheus offered Neo a red pill or a blue pill he said to him. "*You take the blue pill- the story ends, you wake up in your bed believe whatever you want to believe. You take the red pill-you stay in Wonderland, and I show you how deep the rabbit hole goes. Remember: **all I'm offering is the truth**.*" I'm offering all of you a "red pill". Let's see who is brave enough to take it and wake up. And let's see who wants to go back to sleep.

Some have said the civil rights movement was a betrayal, sham, and a con orchestrated against Black Americans by very evil people who called themselves Liberals (now Democrats). The betrayal included using any and every promise imaginable in an effort to hijack two million dormant Black votes in the South, then using them to take over the Democratic Party and the rest of America. To what end? To drive all Christian values from America and then use America's power to implement their sadistic views worldwide. They did this by infiltrating and then compromising the three foundational institutions of the Black community: the **Black preacher**, **Black civic organizations,** and the **Black politicians**. I call this trifecta: "***the Iron Triangle.***"

Sadly, the evidence tilts heavily in favor of this charge. In his Pulitzer Prize-winning book *Parting the Waters* Taylor Branch wrote that in 1956 the Communist Party or Liberals in Moscow ordered their agents in the civil rights movement to establish a "*separate national development for American Negroes, modeled on the Soviet republics.*" It seems to have worked magnificently well, because in 2019, the Black community is the only community in America that has the characteristics of the former Soviet Republics, complete with one-party rule, forced compliance, extreme poverty, government dependency, and dictator worship. If untrue, these Black Soviet-style ghettos that are disrupting and terrorizing America are an amazing coincidence. Nevertheless, one thing cannot be disputed: this was a terrible trade. Blacks gained the right to eat and use the bathroom beside Southern Whites while White Liberals gained control of a nation and potentially the world.

This book explains the hidden history and hidden motivations behind the greatest episode of continuous abuse and betrayal in world history: the abuse and betrayal of Black Americans and America by the Democrats and the Iron Triangle. To maintain 90 percent of the African American vote, it explains how they exploited, not cured, the Stockholm syndrome suffered from slavery through Jim Crow and the paralyzing cognitive dissonance that took its place soon after. It will shatter the lie that White Christian Conservatives are the enemies of Black Americans and expose the Iron Triangle as the Snake in the Garden not whispering, "ye shall be as gods," but screaming "I will make you equal to our god: The White Man". The Primary reason for the fomenting of racial tensions by Democrats and Liberals is to ensure the continual enmity and division among Black and White Christians—because a house divided against itself cannot stand. While Christians fight, Liberals are using the economic and military power of America, not to export Democracy, but to export their immoral ideology to every corner of the world.

OVERVIEW

NOT ALL BLACK preachers, Black politicians, and Black civic organizers are bad—just the vast majority. The present condition of the Black community bears witness to this fact. It is axiomatic: You cannot pick bad fruit from a good tree. Most of them are either immoral, incompetent, or extraordinarily stupid. Either way, they must be exposed and neutralized, not for the sake of Black America but for all of America. Cancer survives in the body because it can disguise itself and white blood cells cannot recognize it. But there is a treatment called CAR-T(Chimeric antigen receptor T cell) that give white blood cells the ability to recognize the cancer cells and destroy them. The Iron Triangle is a cancer that hides in America. Jesus called them "wolves in sheep's clothing". This book will give them a literary CAR-T treatment. I will make them recognizable as the cancers they are. Then we will neutralize them.

Gunner Myrdal stated, "The Negro in America will always be used for either entertainment or exploitation." Like the plantation owners, drug dealers, and pimps throughout history, the Iron Triangle has attached itself to the Black community, sucking away its strength but never giving anything back in return. To understand why this book is important,

I believe a brief synopsis of their treachery, insight to their motivations, and a prophesy to their eventual failure is necessary before we commence.

The Iron Triangle is the descendants of an elitist group of Black people who still believe an un-American idea called the "*Talented Tenth*." It was proselytized by the only Black member of the original nine founders of the NAACP, W.E.B. Dubois. Dubois, a card carrying communist, used the term to describe his belief that the most elite Black men, one in ten, should be placed in the leadership of Black America and the rest of Black America should follow. In other words, these Talented Tenth should be our parents and we their children. John Dalberg-Acton's quote: "*Power tends to corrupt and absolute power corrupts absolutely*," seemed to be ignored in this pronouncement. We can no longer ignore it. Free men are not led nor do they wish to lead other men. They wish to serve. However, this thirst for power evolved and morphed into other more dangerous tyrants. All of these people are not stupid but they believe you are.

Let's start with the crowning achievement of Black identity, the civil rights movement. Considering the above statement by the then-president, the Communists, and its almost 60 years of failure to the Black community, one can see why some would call it a betrayal, sham, and a con. Like all cons and shams, the civil rights movement started with lies. Napoleon Bonaparte stated, "History is fables agreed upon." Sixty years later, the Iron Triangle continues to parrot the lies or fables of their masters. One lie stated "racism is Black America's biggest problem" (fear, incompetence and pride are Black America's biggest problems.) Another lie stated it was a "Christian movement" (Jesus Christ never sought the political power to impose his will on anyone and the civil rights movement was 100 percent raw political power). Another lie stated "Black people were not free" (we were all born free). Another lie was "Black people should be more concerned with how they are regarded by Whites, than how they regard themselves" (that way of thinking surrenders all your power). Another lie stated "any individual success enjoyed by any Black person should be attributed solely to the sacrifices of the civil rights movement and not to their GOD, family, or individual effort" (that way of thinking encourages the surrender of the Will). The most toxic lie was that "only government could provide the answer to the problems that plagued Black Americans" (just go back to the plantation).

Every adult person is responsible for their own life and has to own every choice they ever make. The Iron Triangle stands in contradiction to that statement. "*It is someone else's fault*" is their slogan—never mind there have been volumes of books and lengthy studies that all conclude: victimization is suicidal. Any book on self-help, from the Bible to *Power of Now* or any motivational guru from Jesus to Tony Robbins have all demanded that you not be a victim and state you cannot build your emotional life around the behavior of others, empowering their faults (racism, sexism, or prejudices) to control you. Nevertheless, the civil rights movement convinced Black Americans to do the exact opposite. It was as though the civil rights leadership read books with titles like *How to be Unsuccessful* or *Want to Be a Victim: Here are 10 Rules* and took courses in *How to Be A Slave*. Like all victims in this world, Black people that were mistreated, were not mistreated because they were black: They were mistreated because they were weak. This rule rang true then and still rings true today. Frederick Douglass learned this lesson. After defeating his master in hand-to-hand combat a sixteen-year-old Fredrick Douglas realized: "*A man without force is without the essential dignity of humanity. Human nature is so constituted, that it cannot honor a helpless man, although it can pity him; and even this it cannot do long, if the signs of power do not arise.*"

This is not a mistake. If it was, they would have changed direction and tactics long ago. Instead, the Iron Triangle is doubling down on these failed tactics and savagely resisting any call to change direction. Later in his life after recognizing the devastation the Civil Rights Movement had wrought on the Black Community, Martin Luther Kings successor, Ralph Abernathy went to fellow Black Democrats to consider a plan to get Blacks families off welfare and make them self-sufficient. In his book *And the Walls Came Tumbling Down*, he wrote: "I discovered a curious thing:...They liked the idea of a hugh, economically dependent population. The fact that there were third-generation welfare families pleased them." This is a plan. I submit to you that the Liberals are getting exactly what they pay for: the Black vote. They have been retaining more than 90 percent of the Black vote for the past forty years and over 80 percent for the past sixty years—all due to the efforts of the Iron Triangle. Lose 10 percent of that vote and they lose all of their power. Why would they be motivated to change a thing? Members of the Iron Triangle live like kings in the midst of abject Black poverty. They do not care about Black murder, Black crime, Black family, or Black people. They care only for the Black vote. As it was in the past with their Democrat forefathers, it remains now: Black death is collateral damage in this new slave trade.

Why did Liberals target the Black American community? Why did they choose to employ this trifecta? It's simple: most Black Americans had been trained for this. They knew that Southern Democrats had subjugated Black Americans and had treated them like brute beasts. Through the crucible of slavery and the furnace of segregation, the Democratic Party has molded most Black Americans, as the Czar molded the Russians and the Emperor molded the Chinese, to fit the model of their greatest asset: the compliant and obedient servant. This model has survived every demonic incarnation and seems to be as strong as ever.

"Truths" at one time were self-evident: No longer. In this insane culture, I am reminded of a quote from George Orwell: *"In a world of universal deceit, truth becomes a revolutionary act."* The Iron Triangle are a "Post Modern" cabal injected with the poison of subjectivity and the corpse of immorality. Today, the truth in America can get you can get you killed. Accordingly, most Black Americans have abandoned the teachings of Jesus and have acquiesced to every evil Democrat demand, no matter how insane, including: men can marry men, gender can be chosen, you are homosexual by birth, our children are not human and can be murdered and GOD does not exist. Do not forget, Satan is the father of all lies, and these Liberal pronouncements are lies! They've educated themselves into imbecility. Nevertheless, here's the truth: marriage is defined as one man and one woman. Men have XY chromosomes; women have XX chromosomes. Homosexuality manifests itself in behavior. Every person that doesn't have special needs or is over thirteen years old can control their behavior; therefore gay activity is a choice. Life is defined as having growth, metabolism, reproduction, and reaction to stimuli. To stop that is to murder it. And, delusion is defined as: fixed false beliefs that are maintained despite objective evidence and logical evidence to the contrary. Despite these facts and truths only the most elite thinkers in the Black community will have the courage to change. In the meanwhile, sixty years of Liberal and Iron Triangle control has the Black community positioned at the tip of the Liberal spear, with the primary goal of betraying Jesus Christ again and this time crucifying him in America. Why try to kill Jesus? Jesus has been America's only defense against all Liberal/ atheist dogma. Whether it be communism, socialism, or American Progressive Liberalism, they cannot coexist. For Liberalism to thrive, Jesus must die! This book will argue that just as the Iron Triangle obeyed their masters in the Civil War they will obey them in this war.

First of all, the *White Christian Conservatives that bare the most hatred and blame by most Blacks for their present condition, have nothing for which to apologize.* Any man that blames another man for his present failures isn't worth acknowledging. Furthermore, White Democrats have let it be known since 1800 that Black Americans are their property, under their control, and they would rather see them dead than free. The Iron Triangle was invented to help choke them into submission. There is something to the old Southern argument that the Civil War was not about abolishing slavery. Why? Because slavery never really ended. The Southern states were brought back into the Union but slavery took a different form. The Democratic Party remained the masters of most Black Americans before, during, and after the Civil War. The Iron Triangle was there during every manifestation. The Thirteenth Amendment didn't free anyone; it only guaranteed that the government would no longer officially recognize their involuntary enslavement. If a person is in fact born free, as the Declaration of Independence exclaims, how then can government grant them that freedom anyway? Freedom, like life, is a gift from GOD. Government can no more grant you freedom than it can grant you life. Unfortunately, voluntary slavery to their former masters is the station to which many free Blacks ran soon after federal troops abandoned the South just after Reconstruction. The federal government could do nothing. During the Civil War over 600,000 men were killed, trillions of dollars of property destroyed, and thousands of pages of legislation passed. It did not matter. Blacks, being slaves in their own minds, went right back to the literal Democrat plantation. One hundred years later, after all of the carnage and death of the civil rights movement, they stayed on the Democrat plantation. Therefore, White Christian Conservative Republicans, relieve yourselves of any guilt and no longer live in condemnation. Every adult person is responsible for their own lives. Until the former slave affirms, accepts, and takes responsibility for his own freedom, he cannot be helped. This book will argue that the goal of the Iron Triangle is to stop this at all costs.

What is Liberalism? It is the serpent whispering in the Garden, "Ye shall be as gods." It is determinism not objectivity, the idea that everything is to be questioned, the destroyer of institutions. Nothing is absolute; try it all. There is no repentance because there isn't any sin. There isn't any GOD, gender, color, country, or morality. Everything that makes you an individual must be jettisoned. Isn't that seductive? Like flies around a pig sty, Liberalism felt at home in the party that justified slavery, rape, and murder. The question is why would Black preachers, Black civic organizers, and Black politicians be affiliated with such a demonic group of people? Greed, power, and pride.

In the book *The Prince* Niccolò Machiavelli wrote in 1513:

> Among the praiseworthy men, the most praiseworthy are leaders and founders of religions; after them came founders of republics and kingdoms . . . Infamous and detestable, on the other hand, are the destroyers of religion, the wreckers of kingdoms and republics, the enemies of virtue, of learning and of every other act that benefits and honors the human race. Such are the irreligious, the violent, the ignorant, the useless, the slothful, the cowardly.

For almost 500 years Machiavelli has given us the characteristics of a tyrant: they are the destroyers of religions, wreckers of kingdoms, irreligious, violent, ignorant, useless, slothful, and cowardly. This book will prove the tyrant and the Liberal are one and the same. By their fruits you will know them. We all bear witness to their fruits in the Black ghettos of America. For the past four generations, the idea of Liberalism has poisoned the mind of nearly every Black person in America and caused the world to look at them with either pity or disgust. It emasculates every man that believes the ideology. Worst of all, it caused Blacks to hate themselves. It locked America into another type of indentured servitude, where she is consistently attempting to pay an unpayable debt to a creditor that always changes the amount owed. Many Blacks are now inmates, locked in a prison of their own making. The country and well- meaning Whites are trying to treat a disease that is afflicting an uncooperative patient. This irony fuels the Iron Triangle and the Democrats.

Now, almost 60 years since this poison was introduced into their psyche, most Black Americans, regardless of income, education, accomplishment, still believe as Martin Luther King stated in 1963: "The Negro is still not free." This statement had more of a negative effect on the African American psyche than Jefferson's "All men are created equal" statement had a positive effect on the world. Liberals reinforce this lie because they benefit from it. The most adored and wealthy Black actors, athletes, politicians, or business people will still parrot these suicidal effeminate thoughts publicly in the presence of a world that despises weakness. If you tell them they are equal to White men be prepared to get cursed out and potentially assaulted. As a child I remember hearing Martin Luther King Jr. say that Black people should not be expected to lift themselves up by their "*bootstraps*" because "*they are bootless*." Think about what that does to a Black child's mind. I've heard every derelict Black person and poverty pimp around quote that statement with pride, not shame. I've seen it receive thunderous applause from Black audiences. Their belief in the myth of White privilege and their own inferiority will not allow a debate.

Among the majority of today's Black Democrats, there seems to be some sinister, perverse pride in getting "beaten like a slave" by a White man. They seem to brag about it and post images of the beatings on social media for the world to see, scars and all. It is so important to them to have this experience that they sometimes even manufacture the beatings. They then wonder why they are not respected. Ralph Waldo Emerson wrote: "*Society everywhere is in conspiracy against the manhood of every one of its members.*" Society seems to have won out in the Democratic Party. For that reason I cannot sup with them. No man has privilege over me! It is true: people who believe they were born free and those who believe they were born a slave are both right. Like powerful lions that bow to weaker masters, most Black Democrat men refuse to affirm and "take" their freedom. They want to be "set" free.

In his Gettysburg Address Abraham Lincoln called for America to have a "*new birth of freedom*". I now call for the Black community to have a "**New Birth of Manhood.**" Unfortunately, it is impossible to discuss manhood in the Democratic Party. Today Liberals in the Democratic Party assert there isn't any definition to gender; therefore, "manhood" does not exist. Between 90 and 99 percent of all Black Americans support these people and then are surprised that our communities are in chaos. The Iron Triangle promotes this heresy and uses this knowledge to manipulate and control.

Free men and women cannot be Liberal. Christian men and women cannot be Liberal. One's belief in one's own inabilities and the absolute power of the State is necessary for Liberalism to corrupt one's mind. With Liberalism, an all-powerful State and an all-powerful GOD cannot coexist (see Marxism, Leninism, and Communism). If Liberalism continues to expand, freedom—and therefore America—dies. The death of Christianity and freedom are the primary goals of the Liberal. The death of America is a means to this end. Liberalism cannot survive in American without Black support. Hitherto exists a primary fact: the survival of this nation depends on eradicating this disease in the Black community. This can only be done by exposing and neutralizing the Iron Triangle. Christians of every race, color, and nationality must reconcile under the principals we agree upon and set aside our minor disagreements. Jesus said, "A house divided against itself cannot stand." Nevertheless, Christians have been fighting in a burning house and Liberal Democrats are the arsonists. Before Obama they wore masks. They were "wolves in sheep's clothing". Obama emboldened them. The Liberal Democrats and Iron Triangle are no longer hiding as they once were. They now openly support homosexuality, Gay marriage, government funded abortion even after birth, a borderless country, the eradication of Christianity. Now, there are no masks. They are now just "wolves." Christians can no longer use ignorance as an excuse.

Consider the rebellion, division and confusion the LGBTQ community created February 2019 in the United Methodist Church. Their demand that the Church turn against the Word of GOD, by endorsing and engaging in behavior that has been considered by their Church as either adultery, fornication or abnormal for the past two-thousand years, is the epitome of arrogance and pride. They are threatening to destroy the Church if they don't get their way. Ironically the Church will be destroyed if they get their way. Seems like either way he Iron Triangle will get what it wants.

The unholy wedding of Liberalism and the Iron Triangle was held in full view of the world during the 1963 March on Washington. The Black community, being the bride, decided to denounce the culture of their fathers and incorporate the gods and the ways of its Liberal groom. It's axiomatic: when you marry into an evil family, there will be lies at the wedding.

Proverbs 18:21 states: *"Death and life are in the tongue"*. During the 1963 March on Washington, too many Black tongues spoke "death". Dr. Martin Luther King was wrong when he said so eloquently during the 1963 March on Washington "One hundred years after President Lincoln signed the Emancipation Proclamation" that "the Negro still is not free" and they had come to Washington to "cash a check" for their freedom that had been returned with "insufficient funds." These "death" statements signaled the beginning of the Black community's suicidal slide from an all-powerful-GOD based community to a defeated government based community. It is not surprising then that the King monument in Washington DC is a structure completely void of any mention of GOD. It therefore tacitly admits, as we will discuss later, that the "real" Civil Rights Leadership was also void of GOD and controlled by those that denied his existence. These "death statements" are equivalent to Jesus Christ reversing his message from: "The debt of sin is paid. Satan is defeated. Salvation is yours if you accept it" to: "All Christians must go to Satan for their salvation. If he refuses, you must march and protest at the gates of hell until "He" agrees to give it to you". It is a message of absolute powerlessness and it must be pulled up root and stern.

Dr. Martin Luther King Jr. was wrong when he acknowledged, passive aggressively, that something was wrong with "Black skin" when he said he had "A DREAM" that one day his four little children would not be judged by it. This was another "death statement". As a Black man this is personal to me. I cannot be held responsible for and am not concerned about someone else's prejudice or racism. That's their problem, not mine. What's wrong with the color of my skin? I was alive at that time. I, at that time, was defined as a Negro. Therefore, he was speaking for me. He said I "was not free." But there is a problem. I was born free. I am free. How do I know? My parents told me I was born free. Jesus Christ said I was free. And, "He who the Son has freed is free indeed."

The Iron Triangle has given America a bottomless bucket to fill. It is a conundrum. It is a contract where finalization and the satisfaction of services delivered can never be measured or quantified. It is a trap. The extreme sins of Pride and Unforgiveness were the twin foundational pillars of the Civil Rights movement then and the Iron Triangle now. The misdirected Pride, that caused the Iron Triangle to use protest and disruption to force people that hate them to serve them, along with the Unforgiveness that to this day still causes hate, strife and stagnation is the reason the movement failed and will continue to fail. Today's silly Reparations argument is a result of this orbital spirit of Unforgiveness that has infected the Black community through Iron Triangle. In a statement strikingly filled with the sin of Pride and Unforgiveness. Dr. King said in his "I have a dream speech", "There are those asking the devotees of civil rights "When will you be satisfied?.....No, no, we are not be satisfied and we will not be satisfied until justice rolls down like waters and righteousness like a mighty stream." That was just a fancy way of saying "NEVER"!

The Declaration of Independence said we were all born with the GOD-given right of liberty. Ergo: I am free and there is nothing wrong with the color of my skin. Go ahead, judge me by it. Letting other people control your reality is the best way to ensure unhappiness and self-destruction. The "I have a Dream" speech and its deification world over has done more to steer Black Americans back into slavery than the overseer's whip.

I have affirmed my freedom! No matter how loud the Iron Triangle screams, no one can contradict the word of GOD. No other ethnic group in America would have accepted this universal mark of inferiority from one of its "leaders." Washington or Jefferson would have never uttered such treachery. This "reactive" approach to solving problems has been universally condemned by Steven Covey (*7 Habits of Highly Effective People*), Ralph Waldo Emerson (*Self Reliance*), Jesus Christ (Author of The Universe), and has been known to produce disastrous results. It's like telling a person with heart trouble to eat pork and donuts and not to exercise. Any self help book will tell you: Reactive people blame others. They have accusing attitudes, reactive language, and increased feelings of victimization. Their negative energy is generated by that focus. They neglect areas they could do something about and produce evidence to support the belief that they are helpless. They feel increasingly victimized and out of control, not in charge of their life or their destiny. Their paranoia convinces them to blame other people, circumstances, imaginary prejudices—for their own situation. A proactive person knows no one can hurt you without your consent. In the words of Gandhi, "They cannot take away our self-respect if we do not give it to them." It is a fact that reactive Black Liberal Democrats consent to what happens to them. That hurts them far more than what happens to them in the first place. Until they learn they are what they are today because of the choices they made yesterday," they cannot say, "I choose to change." Gunner Myrdal said "all the negro wants from America is to be accepted". That was our first mistake. A freeman does not "ask for acceptance." He demands to be "respected". Because acceptance cannot come before respect but "must" follow after.

If one-party rule and continual subjugation by Democrats is what Black people wanted, they could have saved America the 600,000 lives lost in the Civil War and just stayed on the plantation.

A close inspection of the Declaration of Independence and the "I Have a Dream" speech will give the reader particular insight into how Liberals and the Iron Triangle are attempting to cheat Black Americans out of their part of this American Democracy. In the "I Have a Dream Speech" Dr. King stated that the Emancipation Proclamation, not GOD was a "great beacon of hope to millions of Negro Slaves who had seared in the flames of withering injustice." He mistakenly asserted that the Declaration of Independence and Constitution "guaranteed the unalienable rights of life, liberty, and the pursuit of happiness." These documents guaranteed nothing. The Declaration of Independence stated that to "secure" not "guarantee" these rights governments are instituted among men. The word "secure" means "attach." To whom are these rights attached, the citizen or the government? The citizen, of course—governments cannot secure your rights because they are usually the ones violating them. It is up to every citizen to guarantee them individually.

He then said, "We've come to cash this check, a check that will give us upon demand the riches of freedom and the security of justice." This was another "death" statement. Freedom and security cannot be "given" by a government. It is usually the entity attempting to take it. The very fact that you have to demand it from them should demonstrate that you cannot depend on them to provide it. Freedom and security are ideals that must be affirmed by the individual and protected by the individual. You have no right to ask governments for them and foolish to believe they will provide it. This why government should be small and limited. If I am going to be attacked, I'd rather fight a dwarf than a giant. The check he spoke of was a government check, written by the same people who had enslaved us for four hundred years. Have you ever heard of a creditor presenting a check to a bank where the debtor not only has no money but the creditor is committing fraud by asking for funds that are not owed?

King had such faith in, what was at the time the White man's government, that he believed that they possessed the powers of GOD. He believed that on demand the government could grant to him and us life, liberty and the pursuit of happiness—attributes that can only come from GOD. Sadly most Black Americans still believe the flimflam men and rainmakers that still sell this "dream." Black people are the only Americans forbidden to evolve and are pushed to devolve.

Like a scorned lover in an abusive relationship, Black Democrats resemble stalkers harassing White America. They are forever trapped in 1963, in grainy black and white, devolving from freedom to government dependence, from GOD to secularism, from objective truth to subjective insanity. Too many Blacks are trapped in a time warp, forever marching for jobs and freedom, never satisfied, begging for the love of someone who already loves them or for the love of someone who never will. They are in a time warp, forever being shot with water cannons and bitten by dogs. Forever dreaming, forever demanding that America cash a bad check where both parties committed fraud. Forever waiting. Forever at the bottom.

In *Mere Christianity* C.S. Lewis wrote: "*If you look for truth you may find comfort in the end. If you look for comfort will not get either comfort or truth—only soft soap and wishful thinking to begin with and in the end despair.*" In the civil rights movement they looked for comfort, not truth. In the end they got soft soap. They got despair. Now we must look for truth. We know the truth: this is not working and most Black Americans incorporate cognitive dissonance to avoid the mental anguish that must accompany any corrective action. Therefore, there is never any corrective action.

This book argues that we Americans must agree with the "life" statements of our founders, who were very jealous in confirming the origins of their freedom, and it did not come from Great Britain or the king. In the Declaration of Independence, Jefferson clearly stated that the colonists were "born free" and the right to "life, liberty, and the pursuit of happiness" was granted by GOD and governments help them "secure" those rights and that they needed to separate from the Country of Great Britain because Great Britain had decided to no longer accept that freedom. This freedom is a gift from GOD and affirmed by themselves. These are "life" statements. Words that give purpose and power not victim status to the people that hear them.

In a letter to a friend after the first battle between the colonists and the British Empire, at Lexington and Concord, Massachusetts, George Washington wrote: "The once happy and peaceful plains of America are either to be drenched in blood or inhabited by slaves. Sad alternative. But can a virtuous man hesitate in his choice."

Today, every American still has to make this choice; but many Black Americans still choose mental slavery. Their grown men now protest like slaves (on their knees) and wonder why they are not respected by over half the nation. The Founders would choose death, risk everything, and kill anyone before they'd be slaves. They also believed, rightly or wrongly, that anyone that did not equally fight, die, and kill for their own freedom did not deserve it.

The Black Liberal idea of freedom consisted of the "dream" of being equal, not equal to good White people (Blacks were already accepted by them) but to the Ku Klux Klan and racist Whites. Only fool would want to be "equal" to those people. Consequently, Black Democrats leaders did become equal to racist Whites and became just like their former White Democrat masters, not understanding Tocqueville said freedom and equality cannot coexist (Communists support equality). They became racist, anti-capitalist, violent, oppressive, anti-Christian and cruel, thus substituting GOD'S limitless gift of freedom for another government "bad check."

The Founders and hence Conservatives understood that a gift from government is earthly and would be bartered for handouts, but a gift from GOD has only one acceptable price: your life. Conversely, most Black Americans and Liberals proscribe the genesis of their freedom, as Dr. King did, to government acts and government documents, namely, the Emancipation Proclamation and the Thirteenth Amendment. Thus, Black and White Liberals see their freedom as a gift from government that must be affirmed and realized by government acts and GOD gives nothing. Thus, true gifts from GOD—freedom, life, self-defense, religion, and sustenance—are attributed to government. For this reason when there is an option to bow the knee to GOD or Government, in the Black community, government usually gets the knee. The example has been set by the Iron Triangle.

This idea is fine with Democrats. Like their slaveholding fathers before them, Democrats cannot admit that Blacks were granted their freedom by GOD. To do this would make them equal and Liberalism is based upon one absolute fact: equality does not exist and can only be attained through government. If Liberals admit that Black Americans' freedom is a gift from GOD and that Blacks are born free, that would also mean their dependency on government is misdirected. Consequently, in the mind of Liberals the actions of most Black Americans verify their belief in this inferiority. A belief that our freedoms come from government not GOD and a "reactive" as opposed to "proactive" plan would explain why the civil rights movement failed for Black Americans but was a complete success for Liberals. It explains the failure of sixty years of social engineering and trillions of dollars of government money.

In the *Republic*, Plato said, the well-nurtured child is one "who would see most clearly whatever was amiss in ill-made works of man or ill-grown works of nature, and with a just distaste would blame and hate the ugly even from his earliest years and give delighted praise to beauty, receiving it into his soul and being nourished by it, so he becomes a man of gentle heart." Since its inception the Democratic Party has been led by a group of immoral people consumed with death and madness. Like rodents and fungus thrive in the darkness and filth of a sewer, they thrive in the darkness and filth of politics. When given the option they supported slavery over freedom, death over life, forced segregation over brotherhood, chaos over family, identity politics over merit, lawlessness over order and open borders over sovereignty. They no longer recognize charm, grace and elegance but celebrate, the vile, the grotesque and the abnormal. It's a place where the Iron Triangle fits very well.

Einstein exclaimed, the definition of insanity is: *"Doing the same thing over and over again and expecting a different result."* If that is true, the Black community needs an intervention. They've been doing the same thing for over 200 years. This book is that intervention. "The Iron Triangle" was hard for me to write. So many sacred cows had to be slaughtered. There were so many myths that had to be debunked. I freely admit, I had bowed to all of these sacred cows. I believed all of these myths. I revered the Black preacher, Black politician, and Black civic leaders. It was quite painful to reveal their sins and see their sins revealed. Moreover, I understand the backlash that will emerge when these unpleasant truths are revealed. This takes courage. There is a tremendous amount of pressure to conform in the Black community, with swift and brutal punishment for those that refuse. Ask Kanye West and Bill Cosby. Nevertheless, the people who LOVE you will tell you the truth. Are you strong enough to handle the truth? Here is the truth. If you want to save your family, way of life, and country, it is time for all Christian men to assert their manhood as did the Founding Fathers. Real Christian men can no longer allow the Left, in the Democratic Party, to shame them into cowardly silence. It is time for emasculated men of faith to reclaim their manhood and understand that their families need their love, protection, guidance, and sustenance. It is time for all Christian men to reaffirm that there are absolutes to GOD, gender, family, country, self- defense, and life. Furthermore, these absolutes should no longer be questioned in our presence without a stern rebuke based on our Bible. In Psalm 118:6, David said, "The LORD is on my side; I will not fear: what can men do to me?" Christian Black men can no longer be concerned with White people and how they are seen by them or anyone else. To quote Emerson again: "What I must do is all that concerns me, not what the people think." In our Bible, St. Peter says in Acts 5:29, "We ought to obey GOD rather than men." But Black leaders have programmed Black people to believe that protest is the highest form of citizenship—never mind that the entire object of protest is based upon the sin of PRIDE and your concern regarding how others perceive you and your desire to change it. If protest brought about desired change, Black people would be the most successful race in the country and Asians would be the least. Instead the converse is true.

These are dark times with dire consequences for silence. Jesus said:

"Or else how can one enter into a strong man's house and steal his possessions unless he first ties up the strong man? Then he can plunder his house." The strong Christian men of all races have been tied up for too long. This is especially true for the Christian Black man. It is time to break the restraints.

"I am" is the most powerful phrase that exists, because the word you put after it will determine what you will be. I say, "I am a Christian." I say, "I am a free man.". Conversely, I have heard too many Black men say, "I am oppressed," "I am not free," "I am still a slave." If you pay attention and listen closely you will hear these phrases ringing from the mouths of some of our most prominent Black Americans, and they are repeated by our children and have spread like a disease among the uninitiated. Many of us have died following this wicked ideology. If we strong Christian men refuse to do our duty, the Liberal Left will kill us all.

The Iron Triangle will explain every question a Conservative may have about Black politics. It will answer some questions Blacks may have about themselves. It will explain how Liberals use race to divide the Christian family. Why is the Liberal line of thinking so effective in the Black community? Why are Blacks willing to abandon their GOD for this party? Why are Blacks so unwilling to leave this party? Why do they hate Republicans? What can we do about it? Why is this important to the survival of our nation? This book explains it all.

Be not dismayed; all is not lost. There are still strong men and women of every race that know something isn't right. They are men and women that stand alone outside of politics and mostly outside of religion. They believe in GOD. They work, take care of their families, and pay their taxes. I am reminded of them in the book of 1 Kings 19:14-18 when Elijah lamented to GOD: "I have been very zealous for the LORD God almighty. The Israelites have rejected your covenant, torn down your altars, and put your prophets to death with the sword. I am the only one left, and now they are trying to kill me too." GOD said to Elijah: "Yet I reserve seven thousand in Israel—all whose knees have not bowed down to Baal and whose mouths have not kissed him."

The Democratic Party is the modern incarnation of Baal. They demand child sacrifice. They demand absolute obedience. They deny the existence of the one true GOD and are actively attempting to drive his face from this world. In the Old Testament God appointed Kings to rule over his people. He held the Kings responsible and made his will known to them through his prophets. The Kings many times, to their detriment, would kill, imprison or simply ignore the prophets with whom they disagreed. Today, the "Kings" are chosen by the people. The prophets are therefore sent not to Kings but to the people. I do not consider myself a prophet. It doesn't take a prophet to see the future of a people that every election year, when given the choice, they choose to send their children to schools that have rejected their GOD and seek leadership from a party that murders babies. GOD himself has already delivered the prophesy. In Deuteronomy 30:19 GOD prophesied: "This day I call heavens and the earth as witnesses against you that I have set before you life and death, blessings and curses. Now chose life, so that you and your children may live." Nevertheless, too many Christians "choose" death. Consequently, it is all around them.

I, however, am happy to report that here in America there are also many that have chosen life and we have many more than seven thousand "whose knee has not bowed and whose mouth has not kissed him." They are about to be activated. In the classic book *An American Dilemma: The Negro Problem in Modern Democracy* author Gunner Myrdal acknowledged in 1944 that there was a certain type of Black American that did not submit to the current social order. He called him "the BAD NIGGER!" Myrdal wrote:

> The esteem in the Negro community for the "bad nigger" is another point. The "bad nigger" is one who will deliberately run the risks involved in ignoring caste etiquette, behaving imprudently and threateningly toward White and actually committing crimes of violence against them. Because he often creates fear in the White community, and because he sometimes acts the role of Robin Hood for lesser Negroes in trouble with Whites, he is accorded a fearful respect by other Negroes. He certainly does not

become a Negro leader. He is a race hero and will be protected by them.

There is an irony in the fact that Vince Everett Ellison, a descendant of slaves, is now reminding the descendants of his former masters about the blessings of liberty and extolling them to not be seduced by the lies of socialism and slavery. Because of my stance on these issues I am sure that many will call me a "BAD NIGGER." I will wear the moniker proudly.

America is approaching its darkest hour. I am reminded of 1938 during Great Britain's darkest hour when another Socialist Liberal, Adolf Hitler, and Nazi Germany were about to invade and kill everyone. Prime Minister Winston Churchill gave one of the greatest speeches in world history and lifted his country to victory. This is how he ended his speech:

> And if, which I do not for a moment believe, this land or a large part of it were subjugated and starving, then our Empire beyond the seas, armed and guarded by the British Fleet, would carry on the struggle, until in GOD's good time, the New World, with all its power and might, steps forth to the rescue and the liberation of the old.

In 1863, America was about to lose the Civil War to the Democratic Party. America was to be destroyed. After the implementation of the Emancipation Proclamation, Northern White men were refusing to volunteer. Abraham Lincoln for the first time then called on the services of once-enslaved Black Men. Two hundred thousand—87 percent of all eligible free Black men—joined the Union Army and saved the United States of America from destruction. As Churchill looked to the countries that Great Britain had once enslaved to save it from Nazi Germany, America may again have to call on the descendants of the people she once enslaved, to again save her, from this modern incarnation of the godless Democratic Party and its traditional army of slaves: the Iron Triangle.

The Iron Triangle

"At what point then is the approach of danger to be expected? I answer, if it ever reach it must spring up amongst us. It cannot come from abroad. If destruction be our lot, we must ourselves be its author and finisher. As a nation of freeman, we must live through all time, or die by suicide."

—Abraham Lincoln
January 27, 1838

Section 1

~~~~~~

VINCE EVERETT ELLISON'S MOTIVATION

For we wrestle not against flesh and blood,
but against principalities, against powers,
against the rulers of darkness of this world,
against spiritual wickedness in high places.
—Ephesians 6:12

WHEN I FIRST walked into that prison I was scared to death! Have you ever smelled evil? It was all around me. However, my fear quickly faded and turned into sadness. I was a correctional officer, a rookie assigned to the Kirkland Medium Maximum Security Correctional Institution in Columbia, South Carolina. My assignment was to maintain security, custody, and control of some of the most violent, amoral people in the world.

When a person's life changes forever, they can always tell you about the day they hit the wall or when they had their "eureka" moment. Mine came the day that I walked into that prison and saw hundreds of young men warehoused in cages like livestock. At twenty-six years old, I was near the age of most of them and the same color. Most of these young men were in prison for crimes they had committed against their own Black people. These crimes consisted of murder, rape, drug trafficking, robbery, and assault. Most deserved to be there but any reasonably intelligent person had to recognize that many of these men were young, Black, and poor.

My reflexes immediately kicked in and like any good Black Liberal Democrat I spontaneously hustled to the victim fallback position where White racism and American injustice were the direct cause of every Black man's downfall including his criminal activity. Murder, poverty, rape, AIDS immorality, and family disintegration in the Black community all resulted from White racism and American injustice. I had been programmed to believe such nonsense. Through twenty-six years of listening to lying civil rights leaders, Black politicians, Liberal media, and Liberal authority figures how could I see otherwise? I was so wrong, so misguided, and so sick.

Compared to most of these inmates, I had as much of a Norman Rockwell-type upbringing a Black boy in the South could have, although, up until I was almost nine years old I had lived in a shotgun house with no indoor plumbing. But in 1972 my father and mother, through hard work, catapulted me, along with my six siblings, out of poverty. I went to church every Sunday, was captain of my high school football team, and had gone to college at Memphis State University (now the University of Memphis). Moreover, my peer group reflected my values. I did not nor do I have much in common with the people incarcerated except for age and color. But I did know this: if not for the grace of GOD, a stern father, and a loving mother, there go "I."

The journey to my awakening began in 1993 on the thirtieth anniversary of John F. Kennedy's 1963 civil rights speech. It was being celebrated in the press and transcripts were available in some newspapers. The speech was designed to garner support for civil rights legislation. This landmark legislation had led to numerous marches, speeches, fights, murders, and civil unrest and was supposed to give Black Americans equal access to all accommodations in American society and in theory (along with Brown vs. Board of Education) cure all of our economic and social ills.

On June 11, 1963 I was seven days old when President John F. Kennedy addressed the nation via television from the Oval Office to explain why it was necessary to pass a bill that later became the landmark 1964 Civil Rights Act. He said:

> The Negro baby born in America today, regardless of the section of the nation in which he is born, has about one-half as much chance of completing high school as a White baby born in the same place on the same day; one-third as much of completing college; one-third of becoming a professional man; twice as much chance of becoming unemployed; about one-seventh as much chance of earning ten thousand dollars a year; a life expectancy which is seven years shorter; and the prospects of earning only half as much.

Immediately after reading the transcript I understood that something was not right. My close proximity to the problem via the South Carolina prison system had given me a particular insight. After a little research it was easy to conclude that matters in Black America had only not gotten better, they were much worse. The president had made a crucial mistake: instead of pressing for the legislation because it was constitutionally and morally correct and understanding that government could and should only assist their citizens in securing their freedom, his rationale rested on the erroneous and then new-age belief that government could guarantee outcomes and could replace the individual as the guardian of their socioeconomic future.

He believed that government intervention could guarantee things that only a combination of education, work, risk, morality, and freedom, all activated by personal initiative, could attain. The socioeconomic plight of Blacks to the government in the 1960s was germane only to the fact that their government was guilty of "criminal neglect" and played the role of oppressor instead of protector or assistant.

Accepting the president's logic, one would have to conclude that if Blacks were richer than Whites then there wouldn't have been any need for voting-rights legislation or civil-rights legislation. All of us know that that would be wrong. Therefore, Blacks being poorer than Whites or not going to college as much as Whites wasn't a proper reason for forwarding civil-rights or voting-rights legislation. It should have been done because state and local governments were violating the Constitution of the United States. Period!

White guilt and maybe an elite arrogance had led him to believe that because government had destroyed the Black community it could also rebuild it. It is just as irrational to believe that if a thug shoots a bullet into a man's brain that this same thug has the ability to perform brain surgery and repair the damage. Or it could be something more sinister? A calculated plan by Liberals to take over the Democratic Party by luring millions of latent Black votes into it by using the unattainable goals of equality, social justice, and forced integration as its bait? Liberal Democrats would then control the Black vote through dependency, ignorance, and fear, which produce a psychological trauma more powerful than slavery: cognitive dissonance. On Feb 17, 1968 former SNCC Chairman H. Rap Brown said "The only difference between Lyndon Johnson and George Wallace is one of their wives have cancer". President Lyndon Johnson said, "We'll have them niggers voting Democrat for the next two hundred years." Blacks have been doing it for over fifty years. Maybe he was right.

Consequently, after almost fifty years, trillions of dollars, mammoth legislation, hundreds of marches, riots, and murder, nothing has changed! Except Liberalism, (which couldn't exist without 90 percent of the Black vote) has over taken the Democratic Party and most of this nation. And for all of their help, Blacks have not only remained frozen in the statistics of 1963, but all of America has added other socioeconomic trauma to the equation. Many can argue that things have gotten worse: President Kennedy did not mention drugs, AIDS, incarceration, crime, or family breakdown, because in 1963 they were too miniscule to define as problems. But they are huge problems today.

After four hundred years of slavery, reconstruction, and Jim Crow, I thought we (Black people) had finally overcome. I thought that after Brown vs. Board of Education, the 1964 Civil Rights Act, busing, affirmative action, quotas, the Great Society, and the second Black president (Toni Morrison and most Blacks agree Bill Clinton was the first) "we" had finally "made it." Ironically, the African American "Generation X" generation will be the first generation in American history whose children will have a lower standard of living than their parents. Black Americans thought that gaining the right to vote and putting the Democratic Party in charge of Black America would lead them to peace and prosperity. They thought that if they elected Blacks into halls of government they would be protected from the police; their children would be educated and their rights secured. They believed what I was told which was: if we only integrated, all of our problems would be over.

Instead, a TIME magazine article by Jack White in 1999 said Black men were an endangered species? The same article sites murder by another Black man as the number one cause of death between Black men ages fifteen to twenty-four. Organizations are having summits in an effort to save the Black family. Blacks are still at the negative end of every socioeconomic statistic in this nation. "Black Leaders" i.e., Black politicians, preachers, and educators are living the high life and blame everyone except themselves for this wasteland they've helped create. Some say, "Now that we have another 'Black' President I am sure everything will be fine."

This is all planned. I can say this with some certainty because theses apocalyptic statistics predicting the destruction of Black America have been known for decades. If this destruction and control was not part of the plan they would try to stop it. Instead, on March 16, 2009, NBC News reported that Washington, DC, has a higher AIDS rate than some West African nations, with 3 percent of all DC residents testing positive for HIV (the virus that causes AIDS). Moreover, it is feared that the numbers could be as high as 6 percent since more than half of the people with HIV are unaware of it. To add insult to injury, in the same year the Heritage Foundation released statistics revealing that one in twelve, or 8.5 percent of all Black men living in Washington, DC, will be murdered before their forty-fifth birthday. And worst of all, according to the Center for Disease Control in Atlanta, Georgia, and the Alan Guttmacher Institute, in 2005 African Americans aborted approximately one hundred thousand more children than they delivered alive. In 2013 in New York City there were 24,108 live births contrasted to 29,007 abortions. According to the Center for Urban Renewal and Education (CURE), between 1967-2015 there were 20,350,000 Black children aborted in America. That equated to 48.45 percent—almost half of all Black pregnancies. There were 423,000 in 2015 alone. That equals almost to one Black American child aborted every minute. In a 2015 list of median household income in the United States including 103 ethnic and Native American tribal groupings, African Americans rank fifth from the bottom at ninety-eight. The top four are Indian, Jewish, Australian, and Taiwanese. Isn't it amazing? We never see them marching and tearing down their own neighborhoods.

It has not always been this way. On Feb. 23, 2017, Forbes Magazine reported that by 1905 Tuskegee Institute had produced more self-made millionaires than Harvard, Yale, and Princeton combined. The median income of White men tripled between 1939 and 1960 from $1,112.00 to $5,137.00 but during the same period the income of Black men quintupled from $460.00 to $3,075.00 and the Black poverty rate fell from 87% to 47%. These facts illustrate that before 1960 Black Americans were progressing at faster rate than any racial group in America. The Iron Triangle in the body of The Civil Rights Movement put a stop to all of that. Before 1960, in the midst of extreme material poverty and political exile, Black America, like the rest of America, enjoyed a culture of life. They married, had children, praised GOD, and respected each other. Their economic progress after WWII had outpaced all other American ethnic groups. Prison, divorce, crime, drugs, and laziness were very uncommon. They controlled their own elementary schools, high schools, and colleges. They had their own doctors, lawyers, dentists, and businesses. This was the time of the Harlem Renaissance, the Tuskegee Institute, Morehouse, Spellman, Howard, Fisk, HBCUs, jazz, blues, the Buffalo Soldiers, the Tuskegee Air Men, and upward mobility. Most only suffered from material poverty but the people were proud, strong, and happy. Now they have kept the material poverty, and through Liberalism have added spiritual poverty to the equation. Many older Black Americans that lived during those times will testify that the Black community was much stronger and better off then than it is today and express disgust with the foolishness of our new society. But they are the ones responsible for this chaos.

How did a people graduate from communal and familial stability to a combination of genocide and fratricide in one generation? Why did they betray the party of their emancipation and swear loyalty to the party of their slavery? Why did they shun the culture and heritage of their fathers to plead and beg for the alien culture of strangers? Why did they turn their backs on the truth of Jesus Christ to accept the lies of Satan incarnate?

The year of my awakening was 1993. I was about to find that South Carolina, like the rest of the United States, was in the middle of the greatest prison expansion in world history. Liberalism had created a culture where most Black men had become so antisocial that society had decided to spend billions to put them in cages. South Carolina was going to expand its state prison system from three prisons and 3,375 inmates in 1973 to twenty-eight prisons and twenty-three thousand inmates by the end of the 1990s and Bill Clinton had just passed nine billion dollars for prison construction in 1994 in an effort to incarcerate at least 50 percent of all Black men under thirty in this nation.

Fyodor Dostoevsky said, "The degree of civilization in a society can be determined by observing its criminals." There has never been a truer statement. I observed. I worked at the Kirkland Correctional Institution for five years. I learned that 85 percent of the men there had four things in common: They grew up in poverty, had no high school diplomas, had no religious foundations, and had no father figures. Moreover, the development of much of their early lives was administered under the auspices of the federal, state, and local governments—aka the Iron Triangle. Most of them grew up in government housing, they attended government school, they were nourished by government food stamps, their health was maintained by government health care, they were arrested by government police, and now resided in a government prison—where all of these amenities exist conveniently under one roof. It cost the government over one hundred thousand dollars a year to keep one person poor.

I am no Liberal when it comes to crime and punishment but I am a student of cause and effect. For every action there is an equal and opposite reaction. There is always a cause, a why. I was looking for that why. Why were the majority of Black Americans getting it wrong? How could immigrants with less than ten years in this country achieve so much, yet much of the Black community after four hundred years was in a social, economic, and spiritual free fall?

There is a "critical mass," an antecedent or an inception for every situation. I studied the effects of slavery, racism, evil Republicans along with the White man's conspiracy to destroy us with AIDS, drugs, and guns. Jews, Asians, and every other minority have the same destructive forces around them and are subject to the same racism from White Americans as Blacks but I did not see them incarcerated in numbers even commensurate to their population. Actually, I saw so few that I could count them on one hand.

Why did so many Black Americans participate in their own destruction?

Before I could begin my search I needed to rid myself of all nonfamily entanglements and conflicts of interest. Accordingly, I resigned from the prison system and began my search. I had looked everywhere but inside the Black community itself. When I looked inside, I found that many of our people were suffering from a spiritual sickness—as does anyone that is involved in self-destructive behavior. African Americans are suffering from a plague. It has permeated almost every fabric of our society. It is not being fueled by the White man, Republicans, drug dealers, guns or AIDS. It is fueled by a warped ideology: LIBERALISM. The enemy is within.

In the same way that bleeding and swelling are the effects to a punch in the face, this destructive lifestyle is the effect of the treacherous LIBERAL leadership of most Black trustees in the Black community:

the preachers, politicians, civic organizations, and their Liberal masters. These Black trustees were supposed to look out for the interests of Black Americans; instead, they were seduced by the dark side of American thought: Liberalism. They were supposed to look out for the spiritual, political, and educational well-being of their people. Instead they looked out for their own self-interest and the interest of their Liberal benefactors. Had they lived up to their trusteeship in the same manner as the elders and trustees in the Jewish and Asian communities, our communities and our children would be inoculated and immune against the spiritual disease that began in slavery and is destroying them today. We are still reaping the harvest of what they have sown in America since 1960 when they allowed the Liberal left to highjack the civil rights movement, thereby turning our ministers into politicians, our schools into training grounds of Liberal thought, and our elected officials into rubber stamps for Liberal governance.

The result has been a culture of death and victimization. They have created young Black men who have no fear of God and no fear of authority, young men who have never served and have no understanding of leadership, young men who consider themselves victims and now create victims. They have no love for their fellow man, no hope, and no future. They dehumanize their Black families and have become more of a dread than any night rider the Klan ever produced. The coddling and excuses of Liberals have spawned an apostate.

The fear of Black men has reached a crescendo in this nation. Black America and all of America are balanced on the blade of a knife. This nation is about to reap the whirlwind of a society that has been compromised by their clergy, educational system, and statesmen.

This book explains how the politics of Liberalism in the Democratic Party took control of the African American community by infiltrating the institutions of religion, family, education, politics, and community and causing a state of dependency that has destroyed their ability to resist. It also illustrates they are employing the exact template with the same result to enslave the majority of America. An Iron Triangle is strangling Black America and is now gripping the necks of all Americans. The clergy, civic organizations, and politicians make up the three sides of this triangle. It decimates by destroying the very roots of the individual: the family, the communities and then the nation.

This story is a warning to the rest of the nation. Look closely at the ghettos of America. If you like them you will love America if Liberals retain control.

This educational system in the 1940s and '50s that developed the first Black middle class is now the worst in the industrialized world. The Black minister is now a caricature and a running joke. The Black family, once envied for its resilience and discipline in the face of extreme injustice and poverty, is now in crisis. Liberal leadership interprets this as utopia. They call Black America their greatest success, their prototype, their Picasso. They want to create the rest of America in its image.

My research told me that what we are witnessing not just the destruction of Black America but the opening act in a tragedy that will be called the "Fall of America." Why would Liberals focus so intensively on this poor, weak minority group? They know what Alexis De Tocqueville knew in 1835 when he wrote in his book *Democracy in America:*

> These two races are attached to each other without intermingling; and they are alike unable entirely to separate or to combine. The most formidable of all the ills which threaten the future existence of the Union arises from the presence of a Black population upon its territory; and in contemplating the cause of the present embarrassments or of the future dangers of the United States, the observer is invariably led to consider this as a primary fact.

The success of America is directly connected to the success or failure of Black America. The intellectuals know it, even if Blacks do not. And as Blacks allow themselves to be manipulated by false GODS with false promises, they lend their influence to the powers of darkness that are using it to destroy their nation.

You may say, "That doesn't make any sense. Why would Liberal Americans want to destroy America? If America dies they die too."

Cancers always kill their hosts. It is natural. Viruses, bacteria, and locusts always destroy their hosts. Liberal politics (abortion, alternative lifestyles, family breakdown, euthanasia, and atheism) are death politics, where twenty-four hours a day they meditate on blood. Many of these Liberals can only have pleasure if they cause pain. Convincing good people that their evil was not "evil" but an extension of freedom was their greatest triumph. They wrapped their evil in innocuous names like "choice," "tolerance," and "equality."

Liberals freely admit that their goal is to change America. If Liberals want to change America it would be prudent to examine the one area in America where they have had the most influence. This area is the Black American community. The death of this America and the birth of another very similar to the ghettos of the inner city where the inhabitants are poor, uneducated, and dependent on Liberal elites is their primary goal.

Every successful business, government, and organization conducts reviews. These reviews are designed to determine whether predetermined goals are being met. If they are, the current direction and actions are continued. If not, an inventory is taken and best practices are continued but underperforming areas are tweaked or abolished. The most prudent of all men understand that no man is infallible and no plan survives initial contact. The Constitution of the United States was left unfinished and amendable because George Washington, Abraham Lincoln, Franklin D. Roosevelt, and Ronald Reagan knew they were not infallible. Yet the sacred cows of the civil rights movement believe that they should never be questioned because there is a conflict. The outcomes and expectations of America are not being met but the outcomes and expectations of Democrats and Liberals are excelling beyond their wildest dreams.

The Iron Triangle rings the alarm. Before a disease can be cured one must first know its cause. *The Iron Triangle* explains what Liberalism is, how and why it has infested the Black community, and why and how it will infest the rest of America. It provides evidence that has been hidden from most and suggests strategies to recognize and defeat this enemy with warnings supported by historical fact of the consequences if we fail to act.

But we will not fail. We will defeat it!

Section 2

~~~

DEVELOPING MY IDEOLOGY

THE CON GAME EXPOSED

Being a Christian and Democrat can be confusing. As I mentioned before, in 1995 I resigned from the South Carolina Department of Corrections and started the African American Unity Congress in a quest to educate Black lawmakers, Black preachers, Black civic organizations, and the Black community about conditions in the ghettos, prisons, schools, and families and ways to change it. Of course, it was the fault of the racists, those evil Republicans. Of course, the Black "leaders" couldn't know, because if they did they would have done something about it, right? I attempted to educate them about the benefits of school choice, welfare reform, prison reform, and independence from government. I wanted to educate them on the evils of abortion, alternative lifestyles, the destruction of family, and the destruction of religion among their constituents. It was the biggest waste of time in my life. They already knew. The Iron Triangle had been active and operating in plain sight for decades. They were orchestrating all of the destruction and chaos in the Black community for their Democratic Party masters.

My next move was to join the organizing of the Million Man March. To me the march had nothing to do with Lewis Farrakhan or the Nation of Islam. To me, it was a rebellion against the current Black leadership in America. After all, the Nation of Islam politically agreed with most of our points. We believed, after the March, that Blacks were going to kick out their current leadership and replace it with one that adheres to the needs of its Black constituency. Nevertheless, after the March, the leadership of the Nation decided to integrate and become part of that compromised Black leadership. After that I understood protest was a sign of weakness and is a pyramid scheme designed to empower only those at the top. I disaffiliated my group from the Million Man March Committee and we continued our fight alone. This split made news all over South Carolina. Consequently, it closed one door and opened another.

A newly elected young congressman one hundred miles away in Greenville, South Carolina, called me and asked if he could come calling. His name was Bob Inglis and he was a Christian Conservative Republican. He and his staff drove the distance from Greenville to Columbia, South Carolina, to meet me and my staff. During a private conversation with Congressman Inglis he confided that he and his staff had been aware of our efforts. We then discussed my political affiliations. I told him that I was a Democrat. Then, point by point he asked me where I stood on the issues of the day: abortion, gay rights, taxes, school choice, welfare reform, family values, prayer, religious freedom, gun rights, and crime. On each of these issues I came down on the Conservative side. I exclaimed, "Oh my GOD I'm a Conservative." What's worse is I had been aiding the enemy.

I felt like Saul on the road from Jerusalem to Damascus. Having been an apostate who converted, I knew what I needed. I was you. You need someone to help guide you through the noise, as Congressman Inglis helped me. You need someone who was lied to and misled, as you are, to help you understand. You need someone who will understand your reluctance and fear to speak out. But also you need an example and reassurance that you are not alone. There are consequences to lying to the strong, and there is about to be a reckoning.

Poverty and Race Are Not the Problem

"Our Constitution was made only for a moral and religious people. It is wholly inadequate to the government of any other."

—President John Adams

"A democracy cannot exist as a permanent form of government. It can only exist until the voters discover that they can vote themselves money from the public treasury. From that moment on, the majority always votes for the candidate promising the most money from the public treasury, with the result that a democracy always collapses over loose fiscal policy followed by a dictatorship. The average age of the world's great civilizations has been two hundred years."

—Alexander Tytler

In his stand-up routine, the late comedian Richard Pryor described how every nationwide social epidemic in America began in the Black ghetto. With Whites viewing it as a treatise to Black depravity, they responded with either apathy or disgust. Then some years later, seeing their children engaged in the same behavior, they would scream, "Oh GOD it's an epidemic." Back then the epidemic was drugs; now, it has expanded to other areas previously believed to be problems of the inner city and quarantined in the ghettos. Even President Barack Obama admitted on January 27, 2014, in an interview with the New Yorker magazine, "The pathologies that used to be attributed to the African American community are now seen in larger numbers in the White working-class communities." This dynamic was also highlighted in a January 5, 2011, opinion editorial for the *Washington Post* by Harold Meyerson titled "America's Downward Slide." In the piece Mr. Meyerson writes:

> The social pathologies long associated with the inner-city poor, single-parent households, births out of wedlock, drug, and

alcohol abuse now stalk the White working class in rural and post-industrial regions far removed from big cities. The middle is falling. Rich Lowry, editor of the Conservative *National Review*, has noted that as wages and employment levels have fallen for the Americans who have graduated high school but not college, their level of out-of-wedlock births (44 percent) has approached that of Americans who haven't completed high school (54 percent). Americans with college diplomas or more, by contrast, have a rate of just 6 percent . . . The great sociologist William Julius Wilson has long argued that the key to unraveling the lives of the African American poor was the decline in the number of "marriageable males" as work disappeared from the inner city. Much the same could now be said of working-class Whites in neighborhoods that may not look like the ghettos of Cleveland or Detroit but in which productive economic activity is increasingly hard to find.

Mr. Meyerson is correct in recognizing the connection between the socio-pathology in parts of Black America and the rest of America. That is the Liberal plan. But in order to assume that poverty is the cause of the pathology, one would have to assume that during the time that most Black families were stable, the majority had to be wealthy or at least middle class and they weren't. In the midst of extreme poverty, depression, Jim Crow, and segregation the majority of Blacks married, remained married, and stayed out of jail.

Crime, family breakdown, and drug abuse are a result of Black Americans' acceptance of Liberalism, not a poor economy. Because this is what Liberals want. If this is not their desired intention, why are they doubling down and expanding and not changing their policies that lead to the destruction of so many people? The disease of Liberalism in some areas convinces a person that what he sees as his problems and challenges are caused by capitalism, religion, and an unjust government. He is taught that he is a victim and can only be made whole by transferring his freedom to a small group of elected Liberal elites that promise to feed, clothe, house, and protect him. This ideology destroys the spirit, the soul, initiative, and provides needed excuses to explain why these actions are proper. Even in the midst of relative prosperity, most Blacks still fall victim to this sick mind-set.

A perfect example of the myth that poverty is the precursor of societal destruction is the conundrum of Prince George's County, Maryland. Prince George's County is the wealthiest majority Black county in the United States and probably the world. According to Data USA the median income of Prince George's County was $79,184 per year compared to $59,039 nationally and $30,134 for African Americans. For decades after the civil rights movement Prince George's County has been consistently violent. According to Wikipedia, it made up 20 percent of all of the murders in Maryland from 1985 to 2006. A twenty-year crime index trend study provided by the Prince George's County Police Department Information Resource Management reported a 68.2 increase in crime from 1984-2004 and a 23.1 percent increase from 2000-2004. If poverty was a precursor for crime, Prince George's county would be paradise. Instead, it is the wealthiest Black majority county in the world and has the same problems with education, crime, and drugs as any welfare ghetto. It averages over one hundred murders a year while its mostly White neighbor counties count fewer than ten. 2017 was a good year; they had only seventy-nine murders. It was time to celebrate. Its schools are below average while the rest of Maryland except Baltimore constantly ranks number one in the nation. In June 15, 2008, in an article for the *Washington Post,* Daniel de Vise wrote about the Prince George's County School system:

> The official graduation rates published by states and school systems are widely regarded as inflated and unreliable. Many in the field have come to rely instead on the annual Diplomas Count report from Editorial Projects in Education, publisher of the trade newspaper *Education Week.* The report estimates how many students in ninth grade graduate on time with their class, using a series of calculations that measure attrition from one grade level to the next . . . The group's latest report, released this month,

showed graduation rates among local school systems range from a high of 93 percent in affluent Loudoun County to **57 percent in high poverty Prince George's County**.

Note: For Liberals to explain the educational disparity, they had to describe Prince George's County as "high poverty," which is an absolute lie. In 2017 poverty was described by the US Department of Health and Human Services' poverty guidelines as a family of four earning less than $24,600 per year. As stated before, Prince George's County's median income is $79,184. Recently, in 2017 it was discovered that the school system is worse. On November 3, 2017, WUSA9 reported that an audit by the state of Maryland found grade inflation and irregularities in grade changes and the manipulation of transcripts after graduation.

The argument that race is a precursor to poverty and crime was debunked in an article written in OZY.com. I was illuminated to find that Nigerian immigrants are the most successful ethnic group in America. If race or color was a factor when determining success in America, how could this be? It is simple. These first generation Africans have not been infected with the disease of the Democratic Party's Liberalism. The June 7, 2018, article written by Molly Fosco explained that today 29 percent of Nigerian Americans over age twenty-five hold graduate degrees and have a median household income of $62,351 per year. According to Quor.com, 41 percent of all Black Ivy League students came from an immigrant background (Africa/ West Indies) even though Black immigrants constitute only 8.7 percent of the population of Black people in the US.

The Iron Triangle remains effective in America because they have convinced most Black Americas that racism and poverty are the cause of every Black problem. Liberals are not stupid: They believe you are. They know the truth and will consistently hide the three deadly diseases they've planted in the Black community. I call it F.I.P.: FEAR, INCOMPETENCE and PRIDE. Fear: Most Blacks are so insanely afraid of racists and racism that the mere accusation causes hysteria and paralysis. Incompetence: The inability to enjoy life, build a family, build a relationship with GOD, recognize evil or make a living. Pride: Too stubborn to change or admit error

The greatest sin committed by the Iron Triangle against its Black victims is not that they expect so little of them but they have trained them to expect so little from themselves. If there were over one hundred murders in any given year in mostly White Montgomery County, Maryland, or mostly White Loudoun County, Virginia, and the schools had a 57 percent graduation rate, there would be Martial Law in these areas and every elected politician would lose their job. However, in the Black community it is to be expected and by the continuation of Liberal social policies and apathy some can say encouraged.

What is the problem? Why do Blacks accept the duplicity? They have blind allegiance to the Democratic Party and the Democrats have accepted Liberalism. To accept Liberalism one must first accept that one is either superior or inferior. If one believes themselves to be superior they expect crime and pathological behavior from their inferiors. And once one accepts their inferior status, they expect and accept pathological behavior from themselves and foolishly expect their superiors to save them. But this leads to another conundrum. Prince George's County is filled with Conservative Christian Blacks but led by godless Liberal politics and politicians who encourage this destructive ideology. Liberalism is a disease that always has and always will destroy Conservative Christians no matter their socioeconomic status. Liberals will never admit to their complicity or to being godless. They have no motivation of ever correcting their behavior. Nevertheless, facts are stubborn things.

As previously noted, this downward decline started in the mid seventies with the maturing of the first Black generation that completely immersed itself in the false doctrine of Liberalism. Led by the Iron Triangle, they were the first generation where too many were not ashamed to be on welfare. They were the first generation where too many relied on government not GOD and family for their security, education, and sustenance. They were the first generation where too many believed that because of past discrimination they were entitled and shunned the concept of delayed gratification, hard work, and personal responsibility. The real danger to this nation rests in the fact that it now seems that elements of

White America are now equally immersed in the same lie with equally devastating results. To add a sense of moral absoluteness to their cause they hire veterans of the civil rights movement as their standard bearers. Instead of being a harbinger of dark times and societal breakdown, currently this dysfunction is considered a virtuous part of Black American and now American culture and folklore.

Too many people become democrats because they want "FREE-STUFF". I'm a conservative bcause I demand "FREE-DOM".

ARGUING WITH ICONS

In the 1940s my paternal great-grandfather P.D. Bond was murdered on the orders of a White man. A Black man named Lee Forrest killed him. Legend has it that his murder was the result of a love triangle, where a Black woman was going to leave her White lover for my great-grandfather, who was a widower. This White man gave the order to "his nigger" Lee Forrest. Forrest lay in wait for my great-grandfather after nightfall and shot him through the heart. My grandmother kept a hope chest. In it, among other things, she kept a handkerchief carried by my great-grandfather the night he was murdered. It was stained with his blood. I asked my father, "Why did Lee Forrest do it? Was it money? Did he hate my great-grandfather?" My father said, "No, back then Black folks did what White folks told them to do."

Times have not changed. History records that racist Whites have always used opportunist Blacks to control the Black masses. The current crop of Black leaders is a variation on an old theme. Lee Forrest killed my great-grandfather by the order of a White man. The Black politicians and leaders are killing the Black community by the orders of White Liberals, like Jewish collaborator Chaim Mordechai Rumkowski in the Lodz concentration camp who assisted the Nazis in the subjugation and murder of the Jews, his own people, for personal gain, even supervising the deportation of children to the gas chambers and the Vichy French during WWII. These traitors know exactly what they're doing.

The credibility of Liberalism among the young is difficult to counter with the presence of Black heros and icons of the civil rights movement more than willing to transfer their talents and voice to support what many have said is an unholy, evil, and immoral ideology. But to be fair, not many Southern Conservative Christians before 1950 were friendly to their Black Christian brothers and sisters and that really hurt Black people's "feelings." Being accepted by nonracist Whites was not enough. Separation from their racist White neighbors was "unbearable." I consider this way of thinking by Black Americans during this time as prideful, envious, despicable, unChristian, and unmanly. Christian men and women should no longer concern themselves with how they are viewed by people filled with hate. We should love them but not care whether or not they love us. Their hatred is their weakness. It is also infectious. The Black community's time amongst these people has caused many of them to reflect their animalistic values. Black people did not change the racist. The racist changed too many Black people into their very image, with one caveat: they're still in blackface.

Sadly, the way they are viewed through the eyes of racist Whites is the most important thing in the world to most Black Democrats. This inferiority complex resulted in Black Americans partnering with groups that made up Progressive/ Liberal politics to achieve power. Liberalism, consisting of a loose group of Communists, Socialists, gay activists, labor unions, feminists, and atheists could not break into the mainstream of American politics. Liberal/ Progressives could loosely be described as any person or group that considers itself as either anti-Christian, anti-capitalist, anti-White, anti-male, anti-establishment, or a combination of those extremes. Using the ancient logic of "the enemy of my enemy is my friend" they concluded that they and many in the civil rights movement suffered from the same oppressor. They, therefore, infested the leadership of the civil rights movement and hitched a ride on the back of its moral absoluteness to force its way into American politics, then into American public schools and then the American mainstream. They even set up affirmative action programs that guaranteed the same White Democrats that hate Black Americans would choose Black leadership. That is genius.

Stockholm Syndrome
&
Cognitive Dissonance

They were going to kill my paternal grandfather. The Haywood County, Tennessee, chapter of the Democratic Party and their military wing, the Ku Klux Klan, had put out a decree: any Black sharecropper registering to vote in the 1960 election would be evicted from the plantation where they resided. Any that tried to vote after eviction would be killed. My grandfather Walter Clark had defied them.

He was almost sixty-eight years old at that time and had been raised in the Jim Crow South his entire life. He and his wife Hattie had taken on the responsibility of rearing my father after my father's mom and dad divorced and left the South to find work up North during WWII. Consequently, my father, me, and all of my siblings were born in Haywood County, Tennessee. The Klan had already seen to it that Walter was evicted. Thus, my father, he, and my grandmother were residing in one of the tent cities set up by the sympathetic Whites and the NAACP. This chapter and tragedy in African American history is well documented in the books *Before the Mayflower* by Lerone Bennet Jr. and *Parting the Waters: America in the King Years* by Taylor Branch.

The Fifteenth Amendment had given Black men the right to vote on February 3, 1870. The Nineteenth Amendment had afforded the same rights to women on August 18, 1920. Because most Black men were not prepared to kill, fight, destroy, and die to affirm their freedom and the freedom of their posterity, my grandfather's newfound voting privilege was made possible because the federal government had passed the 1957 Civil Rights Act. Since Black men would not protect themselves, this Act set up certain federal " *protections*" for Blacks in the Southern United States who wanted to vote. This act was suggested by the Republican Party led by President Eisenhower and Vice President Nixon, NAACP, SCLC, CORE, and other organizations. The Democrats led by then-senators John F. Kennedy and Lyndon Johnson were vehemently opposed to it. Acknowledging the past history of slavery, murder, rape, and assault against Black Americans, Democrats believed that every Black person would vote against them. Therefore, they did all they could to make sure that this civil rights bill would be as weak and unenforceable as possible.

After the evictions and understanding that Black citizens faced death for merely practicing one of their GOD- given rights guaranteed by the Constitution, the president and Vice President Nixon sent John Doar from the Justice Department to Haywood County to brief the Black citizens on their constitutional rights and a contingent of FBI agents to enforce the law, overturn these illegal evictions, and protect the share-croppers against the dreaded KKK. Of course, most Black men would not protect their own communities.

Many times father has told me the story of when the FBI arrived at the plantation where they worked and told them that President Eisenhower and Vice President Nixon had sent them, to my grandfather, that he did not have to move, and they were there to guarantee his and my grand-mother's right to vote. He told me of the pride my grandfather felt that the president was actually concerned about his welfare.

Nevertheless, after four hundred years of slavery, segregation, and hate from Southern Democrats, on the first Tuesday in November of 1960 my grandfather cast his first vote for the entire Democratic Party ticket. John Kennedy and Lyndon Johnson had defeated Richard Nixon with the Black votes Nixon had registered. As a matter of fact, the Democrats won almost 80 percent of the one million newly voting Black Southerners. In all the years I heard this story, the climax made perfect sense, especially with the lies I had been told throughout my life that the Republicans were the villains during that time. After finding the truth the story car-ried a different meaning. My grandfather knowingly voted for the party of the Klan and the party of his oppressor. Why?

I will answer that question with another question: if the slaves at Thomas Jefferson's Monticello Plantation had had the opportunity to vote in the 1800 presidential election for either abolitionist John Adams or their master Thomas Jefferson, which candidate would have gotten the majority slave vote? I can guarantee you it would have been Jefferson. Like religion, language, and food this mind-set is perpetual. It still exists among most present-day Blacks.

Liberal historians will plant a lie into the psyche of America. They will record that Black Americans voted for JFK, LBJ and have remained loyal to the democrats because democrats supported Civil Rights Legislation and turned against Republicans forever because Barry Goldwater did not. If that logic holds true, then Blacks would have voted 80% for Nixon in 1960 and 1968 because Nixon and Eisenhower passed two pieces of Civil Rights legislation in 1956 and 1960. But Blacks didn't vote for them because Nixon and Eisenhower were not democrats and LBJ and JFK were. Black Historian, John Hope Franklin, wrote how the Black votes for Democrats in 1952 guaranteed their dominance and a "survey of the vote in predominantly black districts revealed a majority for the Democratic candidate". Black Freedmen with Stockholm syndrome have been voting for former Democrat masters since Reconstruction.

Most southern Black people were psychologically and physically dependent on southern whites for everything. Southern Whites decided which Black people lived and how well they lived. Blacks believed this and in their struggle to survive, psychologically bonded with their captors. This is the very definition of Stockholm syndrome. Their lives and the lives of their children rested on how well they pleased their White benefactors. Southern Blacks did not hate Whites. Most wanted to be White and part of being a southern White person was to be a democrat. Southern Whites hated Republicans. Therefore, southern Blacks also hated republicans. The fight for Integration highlighted the primary desire to evolve from an undesirable Black culture into the most desirable White culture. It would stand to reason, if southern Blacks fought, bled and died to integrate with Whites socially they would do the same to integrate with Whites politically. Being kicked off the plantation for a little while was a small price to pay if one could peep into that White club just for a little while, even if it was by force. Like all stalkers say: "If you let me in, I promise I won't hurt you. I just want to love you."

After sixty-eight years of oppression and subjugation in order to survive my grandfather had learned to identify with his oppressor. This is not strange. It is expected now but was not fully understood back then.

Democrats and Republicans were more surprised than anyone. Democrats were elated. Republicans called it the "great betrayal".

My grandfather and most of the Black community were suffering from Stockholm syndrome and cognitive dissonance—and still are.

In the pre-Civil War, antebellum South slavery/ western movie, *Django Unchained*, the plantation slave owner, "Master Candy," regarding the docility and obedience the hundreds of slaves on his plantation have toward the relatively few Whites there, asked this question: "Why don't they kill us?" Knowing nothing of psychology, Master Candy erroneously attributed the slaves' docility to a peculiar abnormality that was present only in the brain of the African. Nevertheless, then just as now, it was a matter of curiosity why Black Americans obey and bow to White Democrats when they are obviously oppressing and destroying them as a people.

If you spend any time with any Black Christian Democrat and the conversation inevitably progresses to the troubles in their life, they will tell you, "GOD is in charge of my life." They will without doubt start quoting scripture: Isaiah 54:17, "*No weapon that is formed against me shall prosper,*" or Romans 8:31, "*If God be for us who can be against us?*" Then, in the very next sentence, they will talk about how impossible it is to get anything done because of racism: "Let's demand free health care, food, housing, protection, and money from the government"; "I don't how I'm gonna make it"; "The system is fixed"; "I can't make it no matter how hard I try"; "I'm still not free"; "I want equality!"; "Lets march for change"; "Let's protest"; "Let's riot." The Law of noncontradiction states, "*contradictory proposition cannot both be true.*" Either GOD is in charge and he is your sustenance and nothing can harm you or the White man is in charge and you are still a slave. To hold both of these thoughts simultaneously is classic cognitive dissonance and causes extraordinary mental pain and social upheaval cannot be helped.

We've had this social phenomenon where Liberals are demanding that Southern state governments take down all relics and reminders of the old Confederacy. This entire argument highlights the double-minded schizophrenic mind-set of Liberals and the Black community. I am a Conservative and want limited government because I believe these governments are racists, unfair, and corrupt. I do not trust them. I will protect my right to defend myself against them and, via tax reductions, starve them of the capital they need to do me harm. On the other hand, Liberals believe these same governments are racist, unfair, and corrupt. Nevertheless, after all of the evidence to the contrary most Black Americans still trust these people with their very lives. They insist that these racist, unfair, and corrupt governments be given more power to do them harm and insist on not just disarming themselves but everyone else in America leaving us powerless to resist. This is one of many reasons I consider Liberalism insanity.

I was reminded of Stockholm syndrome and cognitive dissonance after hearing the stories of Elizabeth Smart and Stacey Dugard.

Stacey Dugard was kidnapped by known sex offender Phillip Garrido on June 10, 1991, when she was eleven years old and held captive until August 25, 2009. During this time she was constantly raped and held against her will and gave birth to two children. However, while visiting with Mr. Garrido at his parole officer's office and being questioned privately about her relationship with him she lied and covered for him. She said her name was Alissa and she was a battered wife that was visiting from Minnesota and hiding from her abusive husband. She became defensive and belligerent and demanded to know why she was being interrogated. She only admitted she was Stacey Dugard after the police arrived and Garrido confessed. Psychiatrists diagnosed she was suffering from Stockholm syndrome and later from cognitive dissonance.

Elizabeth Smart and Patty Hearst were also kidnapped and aided and sided with their captors. This is not strange behavior. In these situations it is strange if one is not affected. The Black experience in America is very similar. This is an explanation not a condemnation. It is an explanation.

According to D. Graham PhD & E. Rawlings PhD, Stockholm syndrome is defined as a syndrome where one bonds to one's captor (abuser) in a survival strategy for the victim. This strategy was labeled Stockholm syndrome after a hostage situation in a bank robbery in Stockholm, Sweden, in 1973. Three women and one man were held hostage for six days by two men. During this period the four hostages and their captors bonded bidirectionally. The hostages even came to see their captors as protecting them from the police! Following the release of the hostages, one of the women became engaged to one of the captors, and another of the hostages started a defense fund. All this was done in the face of the fact that the hostages were bound with dynamite and generally mistreated! Such bonding to one's captor/ abuser is no longer considered unusual by professionals who negotiate with hostage-takers. In fact, they encourage its development, for it improves the chances for survival of hostages, despite the fact that it means the officials can no longer count on the cooperation of the hostages in working for their own release or in later prosecuting captors.

Bonding with an abuser maybe the universal survival strategy for victims of interpersonal abuse? Think of the character "Reek" aka Theon on "Game of Thrones" and Darth Vader saying "I must obey my master". They both changed but it was a lot of drama in between.

The brutal conditions of American slavery, where a person's life, health, family, and everything else was tied to their relationship with their master, was a perfect environment for cultivating this mental debilitation. Pleasing the master was essential—not just to their survival but to their very existence. During slavery, revolts were very rare. Retribution against masters was very rare. After slavery, very few freedmen left the South and many stayed with their former masters. This master–slave relationship lasted through Jim Crow until the early 1970s and slowly gave way to a government–slave relationship. Government now controls most Black Democrats' life, health, family, and everything else, with one caveat: the slave now has the option to leave the plantation. He knows he should leave. But this is when cognitive dissonance provides him with every excuse to stay. The snake in the garden whispers in his ear: you cannot go. "Republicans are racist," "Democrats love Black people," "The White man has the game fixed," "They won't give a brother a chance." The Iron Triangle, the snake in the garden, promotes these lies and draws their strength from them.

Studies of other hostage-like groups seem to bear this out. These groups are:

- Hostages

- Concentration camp prisoners
- Cult members
- Prisoners of war
- Civilians in Chinese Communist prisons
- Procured prostitutes
- Incest victims
- Physically and/or emotionally abused children
- Battered women

There are eight situation factors that are precursors to Stockholm syndrome:

1. Perceived threat to one's physical or psychological survival and the belief that the captor would carry out the threat.
2. Perceived small kindness from the captor to the captive. (Note: letting the captive live is enough.)
3. Isolation from perspectives other than those of the captor.
4. Perceived inability to escape.
5. ***Negative feelings by victims toward family, friends, or authorities trying to rescue or support them or win their release. (This factor will be revisited frequently.)***
6. Support the abusers reasons and behavior.
7. Inability to engage in behaviors that may assist in their release or detachment.
8. Supportive behaviors by the victim, at times helping the abuser.

In Aesop's fable "The Fox and the Grapes" a fox is attempting to eat grapes from a vine but fails to reach them. Instead of admitting defeat, which would have caused him mental pain or dissonance, he comforts himself by saying "They were probably sour." This little story is a classic example of cognitive dissonance.

Cognitive dissonance is defined as an uncomfortable feeling caused by holding two contradictory ideas simultaneously. The "ideas" or "cognitions" in question may include attitudes, relationships, and beliefs. "Dissonance" or "discord" usually occurs when a person perceives a logical inconsistency among his or her "cognition" or ideas. This happens when one idea implies the opposite of another—for example, a priest involved in sexual activity or a drug councilor who smokes crack. Noticing the contradiction would lead to dissonance, which could be experienced by anxiety, guilt, shame, anger, embarrassment, stress, and other negative emotional states. When people's ideas are consistent with each other they are in a state of harmony or consonance. Thus, Black Americans have to excuse or justify the abusive and racist behavior of Democrats to avoid mental pain. Because they love the political party that is abusing them they must find another culprit for the crime, their failing schools, and the violence in their neighborhoods—classic cognitive dissonance.

Human striving for internal consistency is the basis for Leon Festinger's theory of cognitive dissonance. When dissonance occurs people have a tendency to feel uncomfortable and set out to reduce this discomfort or dissonance and actively seek to avoid situations and information that may increase it. This explains the vile hatred of Republicans in general and Black Republicans in particular.

There are three ways people may adjust their attitudes and actions. These adjustments result in one of three relationships between two cognitions or between cognition and a behavior.

1. Consonant relationship: Two cognitions/actions that are consistent with one another (Example: Not wanting to buy anything while out, then only eating free samples.)
2. Irrelevant relationship: Two cognitions/actions that are unrelated to one another (Example: Not wanting to buy anything while out, then having a conversation with a friend.)
3. Dissonant relationship: Two cognitions/actions that are opposite to one another. (Example: Not wanting to buy anything while out, then maxing out one's credit card.)

Most African Americans find themselves caught in the dissonant relationship brought on by an irrational and blind trust in the same White

Democrats who enslaved, segregated, and subjugated them and their ancestors for four hundred years and are still doing so. The platform of the Democratic Party and the belief system of Liberalism stand in direct contradiction to everything Christians believe. It also runs counter to the natural reactions one should have to a known enemy. Even if most Black people do not know the platform of the Democratic Party most do have eyes. This explains the disharmony in parts of America and the extreme disharmony present in the Black community.

Reactive people are emotional. Proactive people are more controlled and thoughtful. I have argued that most Black Democrats are extremely reactive and as a consequence extremely emotional, especially regarding politics and their Democrats. Consequently, they consistently make terrible political decisions. Because one thing is certain, there are three areas where you must negate emotion and apply absolute logic: *justice, finances, and politics*. Among most Black Democrats the failure is extreme in all three of these areas but in regards to politics it is gargantuan. Furthermore, the evidence supporting this charge is mind blowing.

The theory of cognitive dissonance is based upon the basic assumption that people seek consistency between their expectations and reality. People will engage in an activity called dissonance reduction in an attempt to bring their cognition and actions in line with one another. If successful this will allow for a decrease in psychological tension and distress. Reduction can be achieved in four ways.

Attitude: *I am a free, intelligent, Christian Black person.*

Behavior: *I vote for the anti-religious Democrat candidate 100 percent of the time.*

1. Change behavior/cognition (Example: Start studying. Vote for the best candidate.)
2. Justify behavior/cognition by changing the conflicting cognition. (Example: All Black people vote Democrat. It's tradition.)
3. Justify behavior/cognition by adding new cognitions. (Example: I will stop voting Democrat when Republicans start showing up.)

4. Ignore/deny any information that conflicts with existing beliefs. (Example: I am a proud Christian Black person and Democrats have always treated Black people well and always take care of us and all Republicans are racists.)

In an attempt to live a life with as little mental pain as possible, most Black people turn to item number four. They ignore or deny any information that conflicts with existing beliefs. I have seen people close their ears. Scream! Say, "I don't want to hear it, I don't want to hear it!" I've seen people sprint away like they were being chased by a ghost just to escape the pain of facing the truth. Some even justify their blind faith by asserting that all Republicans are racist—as if they know all Republicans.

All Republicans are not racist, but what if it were true? Why would it matter? Racists are people of inferior intelligence. I don't care what a fool believes. It only matters if you believe they are superior to you. If you believed you were better or at least equal, another person's feelings about the color of your skin would be of no consequence. Ironically, White men never cared. It didn't matter whether they were minorities in Africa and Asia or the majority in Europe. They did not care that people from other races considered them savage and inferior. Although untrue, they "*believed*" they were superior and heirs of Jesus Christ. Right or wrong they used that faith to take over the world. And most Black men, while still coveting the love of White racists, can't even find the job they desire.

Love the ones that hate you but never covet their love. Love yourself. Love everyone. But care only if you are worthy of the love of your wife and in the will of GOD. Strive for your hater's respect, not their love. If they refuse to give it, earn their fear.

However, most Black Democrats seem to be suffering mostly from a level of cognitive dissonance called "effort justification." Saul McLeod put it this way:

It also seems to be the case that we value most highly those goals or items which have required considerable effort to achieve.

This is probably because dissonance would be caused if we

spent a great effort to achieve something and then evaluated it negatively. We could, of course, spend years of effort into achieving something which turns out to be a load of rubbish and then, in order to avoid the dissonance that [it] produces, try to convince ourselves that we didn't really spend years of effort, or that the effort was really quite enjoyable, or that it wasn't really a lot of effort.

In fact, though it seems we find it easier to persuade ourselves that what we have achieved is worthwhile and that's what most of us do, evaluating highly something whose achievement has cost us dear—whether other people think it's much cop or not!

If we put effort into a task which we have chosen to carry out, and the task turns out badly, we experience dissonance. To reduce this dissonance, we are motivated to try to think that the task turned out well.

This explains why in the Black community there cannot be an intelligent discussion regarding the civil rights movement or politics. Any criticism is met with extreme hostility and anger. There was so much effort, pain, and death put into it that it causes too much pain to admit it did not turn out well. Therefore, we cannot correct it. It has turned into a money pit, a project where so much time and effort has been invested, the investor cannot countenance the loss. So, instead of stopping the bleeding, admitting defeat, and starting again with something that will bring him profit, he continues to throw good money after bad, eventually losing everything. The civil rights movement, The Democratic Party, and Liberalism are all money pits. It is time to stop the bleeding. We have to put a tourniquet on it and begin something more profitable.

Jesus said in Matthew 6:24, "No man can serve two masters. Either he will hate the one and love the other or he will be devoted to the one and despise the other."

Our Bible was speaking of cognitive dissonance and was warning Christians against it. It warned that it was destructive. If one needs proof of this observe the condition of Black America. A man cannot have two masters, loving the one of darkness and hating the one of light. One cannot love Godless Liberalism and love GOD. One cannot love oneself and empower the enemy to rule over you and your family without it resulting in massive mental stress, which manifests itself in destructive behavior. It is after all the "law" of noncontradiction not the "suggestion" of noncontradiction.

James concluded the matter when he stated in chapter 1 verse 8: "A double-minded man is unstable in all his ways."

It must be understood that most Black Americans have a suicidal pact with the Democratic Party, not Liberals or Progressives. Most Black Americans will vote for a Bible-carrying, Conservative Democrat, Blue Dog Democrat, or an Atheist/Jewish/Muslim, pinko Communist Democrat; he or she only need be a Democrat. It just so happens that most Democrats today happen to be Liberal.

Democrats and Liberals took advantage of Black Americans' Stockholm syndrome/cognitive dissonance to lure them to and keep them in the Democratic Party while it was still controlled by White supremacists. The Liberals then leveraged the Black vote to take over the Democratic Party little by little. What else could have caused Southern Blacks to vote for the Party of George Wallace and the Ku Klux Klan except Stockholm syndrome or cognitive dissonance? Liberals then expanded the Democratic Party to include atheists, abortionists, feminists, Socialists, the gay lobby, and unions. They believe every Liberal Democrat crime can be justified by falsely saying the other side is "RACIST" and most Black Americans choose to believe it.

This schizophrenic relationship has led to such disharmony that Black America is in the midst of a fratricidal meltdown. The inability of the victim to assist in their own release and their violent resistance to anyone trying to assistance in their freedom is the most disheartening aspect of the syndrome

This explains why there is so much irrational hatred for Black Republicans. It explains why there is such an intense resistance to help and change while they watch the killing of their children and are mistreated by their elected officials. Moreover, the fact that the "Liberal"

Press has not called the Democrats to task for this desolation reveals that they are in league with the conspiracy.

Stockholm syndrome consists of loyalty to a more powerful abuser—in spite of the danger that this loyalty puts the victim. It is common among victims of domestic abuse, battered partners, and child abuse. In many instances the victim chooses to remain loyal to their abuser and not to leave him or her, even when they are offered a safe placement. This unhealthy type of mental phenomenon is also known as trauma-bonding to the perpetrator.

However there is an additional element in Stockholm that made Black Southerners very susceptible to it. Pierre Bourdieu in his "Five Forms of Capitalism" describes Stockholm syndrome as a dynamic where social action amounts to a type of capital (something of worth), which can be used by the powerful (segregation-minded Whites) for power, in various fields of social interaction (Blacks at the back of the bus, colored water fountains, segregated schools). This power depends on violently preventing others from accessing this capital (voting, eating at lunch counters, education, elected office). In the Marxist class theory, capital is necessary for self-realization. Traditions maintain class society, and even when victims (Black leaders) are put into a position of power they see their abductor in a compassionate way. In fact the victim still has a strong psychological need to be socially equal to his victimizer. This need may be accompanied by a sense of security that exists between the loyal person and the victimizer.

The Liberal Democratic Party lends this capital exclusively to the Iron Triangle. The Iron Triangle uses this capital to maintain power in the Black community. The psychoanalytical view of the syndrome describes it as "an emotional attachment to the nearest powerful adult in order to maximize the probability that this adult will enable—at the very least—their survival."

I once heard a story of an old slave woman who had an abusive master. When the master died the old slave woman was inconsolable. Weeping uncontrollably she exclaimed: "My master is dead. My master is dead. I hope that when I die and go to heaven I can still have him for my master."

As you can see, the Stockholm syndrome existed long before the hostage situation in Sweden. It existed in America between the victim and the victimizer since the 1600s. A derivation of it existed in 1965 and still exists in parts of the Black community presently. The trauma of American slavery is almost impossible for us to imagine. It was so long ago. Everyone that either witnessed or was subjected to it has long since died. But we have all read eye witness testimony and seen films and movies of Nazi concentration camps during WWII. Because of that, we have more of an intimate understanding regarding their plight and understand it as the most evil and traumatic event in the history of mankind. Psychiatrists have compared the treatment of Blacks in American slavery to the treatment of Jews in Nazi concentration camps. Bear in mind: the Jewish people suffered this for approximately seven years and Blacks for over four hundred. The trauma to Blacks must be considerable. It also must be considered that the Jewish people had millions of Jews unaffected by the Nazis who were able to help them recover, be rehabilitated, become reinstituted into civil society, and found their own country. Blacks also had a support system of free Northern Blacks, many of whom had fought in the Civil War. However, the Democrats of that time and their Iron Triangle cohorts betrayed, murdered, and intimidated these men and women and kept the South pristine. The White master needed his cotton picked and the Iron Triangle needed to fortify their position near him. They will remain there as long as they guarantee this support group will never be developed.

In 1965, the Moynihan Report quoted psychiatrist Stanley Elkins comparing the abnormal behavior of the prisoners in Nazi concentration camps to American slavery. He surmised:

Both were closed systems, with little chance of manumission, emphasis on survival, and a single omnipresent authority. The profound personality change created by Nazi interment as independently reported by a number of psychologists and psychiatrists who survived, was toward a childishness and total acceptance of the SS guards as father figures—a syndrome strikingly similar to

"Sambo" caricature of the Southern slave. Nineteenth-century racists readily believed that the Sambo personality was simply an inborn racial type. Yet no African anthropological data have ever shown any personality type resembling Sambo; and the concentration camps molded the equivalent personality pattern in a wide variety of Caucasian prisoners. Nor was Sambo merely a product of "slavery" in the abstract, for the less-devastating Latin American system never developed such a type.

Dr. Elkin's was describing the Stockholm syndrome and connecting that syndrome to the continual effects of slavery toward Black Americans as far forward as 1965. However, Dr. Elkins did not call it the Stockholm syndrome, he called it Sambo because the term Stockholm syndrome was not coined until 1974. Nevertheless, like cancer the disease has existed forever. However, it wasn't given its name and was not completely understood until the 1970s. This could vey well explain Black submission to the Democratic Party in 1960 and their continued loyalty even now.

Examples of this syndrome exist throughout Southern folklore. My father usually relays stories to my siblings and me regarding many of his experiences growing up in the Jim Crow South. In each of his stories lies an intimate knowledge of the culture, of the Black and White dynamic and how Whites kept Blacks economically and socially dependent on them. One of my father's stories consisted of a poor Black sharecropper that had gone into town, gotten drunk, and gotten arrested. Even though I do not remember the moral or the jest of the story I do remember a part that always troubled me. When the poor sharecropper was brought in front of the White judge, the judge, seeing he was Black, would ask, "Whose nigger are you?"

To interpret: the Judge was asking the man, "What White man will come speak on your behalf?" If he had one, they would release him into his custody. If he did not he would have to serve his sentence in the county work house and be hired as slave labor. If the Black man had a White benefactor he would respond "I am Mr. So and so's nigger, sir."

This phenomenon was always present. Why else would Black leaders refuse "freedom" and choose government guaranteed "equality" with their former master? Victims have always proven to be the worst judges of their former abusers. They either destroy them or want to become them. It is logical to assume that this syndrome played an uncanny role in the decision-making process of an abused and victimized Southern Black leadership during the sixties and led them into traps so illogical that a dysfunction may be the only sensible way to explain the folly.

Even today, Democrats will use the fact that they get 90 percent of the Black vote as a fact that Democrats are delivering for Black people. This is the same logic used by slave holders before the Civil War to prove that slaves were satisfied with their condition on the plantations. They would argue: if the Slaves are so unhappy, why don't they revolt?

Therefore, enslavement is justified and even desired by the slave. The Democrats believed it then when Blacks did not revolt as slaves. They surely believe it now when they do not revolt as free men.

Here's the good news: no lie can last forever. Evil will eventually turn on itself and good will triumph. Evil has its reign, and somedays these wretched beasts seem to have the power of the universe at their disposal. With the advent of the internet, social media, and science, the insanity of Liberalism will soon be on full display. Their lies were previously hidden. Newspapers would not print them. The evening news would not discuss them. The pulpit would not confront them. Today they are being exposed. The Liberals will soon start to cannibalize one another.

It was necessary that we live through this time. For the son of perdition to reveal himself there first had to be a falling away. The true people of GOD are revealed in times of trouble and in times of stress. Do not fear these times, welcome them. They are opportunities to display your love and your faith.

COGNITIVE DISSONANCE

Examples of Black cognitive dissonance include:

- The Black community is the most pro-life group of people in American society. Yet they abort more of their children per capita than any other group. There were approximately five hundred thousand Black abortions in the US last year, or one Black abortion every minute.
- Around 82 percent of Black parents believe in school choice yet consistently vote for politicians who fight against it. Consequently, the worst public schools in America are almost unanimously attended by Black children.
- The Black community is staunchly Conservative regarding traditional family values yet divorce is rampant and homosexuality and promiscuity are expanding, which has caused AIDS to become the number one killer of Black men and women between the ages of 18 and 45.
- Blacks are the most religious Christian people in America yet we commit most of the crime in this nation and Black-on-Black murder has become a worldwide phenomenon.
- Many Blacks consistently speak of White oppression, Black pride, Black is beautiful, Black culture, and the love Black men have for Black women, yet many of those same Blacks destroy their own neighborhoods, use the words "nigger" and whore to describe their own people, and consistently fight for forced integration with the people they see as their oppressor.
- Blacks consistently protest against White supremacy, police brutality, and White racism, yet they constantly vote to expand the power of these very same people by asking for more police, gun confiscation, and government control.

The evidence is clear: this disharmony has brought about catastrophic results. One has to admit this is abnormal. Now we must deal with the next series of questions: Why does it continue? How do we stop it?

After the deafening silence behind the tens of thousands of Black-on-Black murders, the hyperbolic reaction of Black America to the homicides of Trayvon Martin, Michael Brown in Ferguson, and Eric Garner because they were all killed by White men is a case study of cognitive dissonance. Among Black leaders, the taking of Black life is only relevant when it is taken by White men. Why? In the mind of the victim, only the actions of the dominate person are relevant. The facts of these cases do not matter. It does not matter that each one of these African American men were involved in illegal activities or that their illegal actions led directly to their deaths. It also does not matter that juries either found not guilty or failed to indict any of the White men who killed them. Like a battered wife pleading for the love of an abusive husband, the only existing issue to a Black Liberal begging for the love of his superior is that he again is being rejected by the people he loves the most.

Traditional Black leadership dismisses the thousands of Black-on-Black homicides because they themselves reject Black Americans. Many prominent Black leaders and entertainers have been heard making very derogatory statements about African Americans only to be invited to the White House and celebrated by an African American president. These men are walking contradictions. Now after fifty years of failure they are doubling down on these flawed positions.

In his book *The 7 Habits of Highly Effective People,* Stephen R, Covey wrote:

> The proactive approach to a mistake is to acknowledge it instantly, correct, and learn from it. This literally turns a failure into a success. "Success," said IBM founder T.J. Watson, is on the far side of failure . . . But not to acknowledge a mistake, not to correct it and learn from it is a mistake of a different order. It usually puts a person on a self-deceiving, self-justifying path, often involving rationalization (rational lies) to self and to others. This second mistake, this cover-up, empowers the first, giving it disproportionate importance, and causes for deeper injury to self

. . . It is not what others do or even our own mistakes that hurt us the most; it is our response to those things. Chasing after the poisonous snake that bites us will only drive the poison through our entire system. It is far better to take measures immediately to get the poison out . . . Our response to any mistake affects the quality of the next moment. It is important to immediately admit and correct our mistakes so that they have no power over the next moment and we are empowered again.

The answer: you must have the courage to know yourself and then vote your values. The Delphic maxim, "Know thyself," is still paramount. Socrates taught: "The unexamined life is not worth living." We must have the courage to admit and correct our mistakes. Black Americans have demand that White America re-examine their history and repudiate every person that supported slavery or racism. It is time for Black people to do the same. Black Americans, especially, must admit that the victimization culture that was and is the staple of the civil rights movement was a mistake. It has paralyzed the Black community and our present condition of extreme poverty and crime are a direct result of it.

William Shakespeare dealt with the mental pain of Cognitive Dissonance when the main character in his play Hamlett eloquently relayed these words:

"To be or not to be, that is the question;
Whether 'tis nobler in the mind to suffer
The slings and arrows of outrageous fortune
Or take up Arms against a Sea of troubles,
And by opposing end them.

In the Declaration of Independence, Thomas Jefferson relayed the same mental pain experienced by the Founding Father and America in the years before the American Revolution when he wrote: "All experience hath shown that mankind are more disposed to suffer, while evils are sufferable than to right themselves by abolishing the forms to which they are accustomed."

It is in our nature to preferably deal with the Devil we know than fight a Devil we don't know. For this reason, only the brave and the elite thinker will heed my call to change. The Founders were the elites of their society. Thus, Jefferson continued in the Declaration: "But when a long train of abuses and usurpations, pursuing invariably the same Object evinces a design to reduce them under absolute Despotism, it is their right, it is their duty, to throw off such Government, and to provide new Guards for their future security."

It is time for Black Democrats to understand as Jefferson understood. These evils will not "right themselves". They must do their duty and throw off this despotic government. It is just as important for Conservatives to understand it is nothing we can do to help these enslaved people until they decide to "take arms against a sea of troubles and by opposing: END THEM!!

It has been done before. Alex Turner was a slave born in 1845 on The Gouldin Plantation in Virginia. This Virginia plantation was a living hell for young Alex for one particular reason, The White master had chosen of Black overseer to keep his more than two hundred slaves under control and producing at maximum efficiency. This Black overseer was one the original members of the Iron Triangle. This overseer made young Alex's life a living hell. When he discovered that young Alex could read he, beat him mercilessly and worked him like an animal. Alex would not forget. When the Civil War started Alex escaped and joined the First New Jersey Volunteer Calvary. In 1863 Alex guided his fellow Black Union Soldiers back to the Gouldin Plantation. The overseer heard all of the commotion outside and stuck his head out of window asking "who's there". Alex Turner responded "It's Alex and I'm gonna shoot you." Alex Turner slew his former overseer.

After achieving his revenge Alex continued to fight for the Union. After the war he did not go back down South. He settled in Grifton Maine where he purchased 150 acres of land married and had 16 Children.

Alex Turner along with Fredrick Douglass, Harriett and the men of the 54th Massachusetts are a few of my heroes. Others may prefer people that were beaten, were shot with water hoses or had attack dogs thrust upon them. I prefer people that fought back. These people saw the truth and ginned up the courage to fight through their Stockholm syndrome and Cognitive Dissonance. They faced obstacles one million times more difficult than any of us will ever face. They had vicious dogs, slave catchers, Confederates and house negroes chasing them. Believe me the Iron Triangle existed and was employing their art of betrayal even then. Blacks now only need to wake up in the morning and make a decision not to be a slave anymore. Sadly, most are too cowardly to even do that.

Are you a Christian? Find out what that is. Fight for it. Live it. Vote it. Are you a man? Find out what that is. Fight for it. Live it. Vote it. Are you free? Find out what that is. Fight for it. Live it. Vote it. Liberals will seek to exploit a contradiction in any one of these areas. And even though Liberal Democrats know the formula to success in America, like the Democratic Party members before them who killed Black slaves for learning to read, they will continue to keep this knowledge to themselves at all costs.

What Do We Believe?

The Devil whispered in my ear,
"You're not strong enough to
withstand the storm."
Today I whispered in the Devil's ear,
"I am the storm."

The cowardly fear that most Blacks have toward White racism is so consuming it has reached the level of narcissism, paranoia, paralysis, and insanity. It is phobic and irrational, like the fear of snakes and spiders. It's paranoid and conceited, like Tupac's "All Eyez On Me." Most are so filled with either fear or self-importance that they believe every White person uses every waking hour plotting against him or her. Believe me Black people when I tell you: the vast majority of White people aren't thinking about you. The only ones that do are the White

Liberals with their feet on your necks.

This irrational fear by Black Democrats has made White Americans GODlike in their eyes. In the mind of most Black Democrats, the White man controls their income, health, education, identity, sex life, drug trade, the weather, who has what, and everything else. The stated goal of most Blacks is to be **EQUAL** with Whites—or in other words, "I want to be like him." The stated goal of every Christian should be: "I want to be like Christ." But in the eyes of too many Black Americans the White American is superior to Christ.

White people are even confused. Most of them do not understand the Black obsession to integrate and be equal with them. Many look at beautiful Black culture and Black people and wonder "Why do you care what we think?" Because most of them do not care what Black people think.

It must be understood: Black Americans cannot control events. They can only control how they respond to them. Trying to eradicate and control racism has been our greatest folly. It's like trying to control the weather. Man did not try to control it. He built houses to protect himself from it. Our houses against racism should be our faith in GOD, our families, our education, our fortitude, our perseverance, and our competence.

The biggest secret in America is in the American economy: ***"Competence and fortitude trumps all racism"***.

White men never concern themselves with how they were regarded by other races; other races were concerned about how they were regarded by White men. That is why they took over the world. If you want to emulate and learn one trait from your White brothers, learn from or emulate that one.

On March 26, 1974, Muhammad Ali was in Caracas, Venezuela, to perform the blow-by-blow color analysis for the George Foreman vs. Ken Norton Heavyweight Championship fight. Before the fight famous boxers in attendance were asked to come into the ring and were introduced to the audience. One these boxers, Oscar Bonavena from Argentina and a favorite son of South America, received a thunderous ovation. Ali and Bonavena had history. They had fought on December 7,1970, in a vicious fight where Ali TKO'd Bonavena with only seconds left in round

15. Bonavena was still angry. While in the ring in eyeshot of thousands of people in the auditorium and millions of people on television, Bonavena took off his jacket, pointed at Ali, called him a coward, and dared him to come into the ring. Ali immediately left the desk where he was conducting his job as play-by-play announcer, ran up to the ring apron where he was visible by the TV audience, and started screaming at and jabbing up at Bonavena, who was still in the ring pointing down at him. The crowd saw the commotion and started screaming with excitement. After things quieted down and Ali returned to the microphone he apologized to the audience. He said, "I can't have a man come threatening me like that. He don't threaten me. I'm the Threatener."

This why Ali is a legend. While other Black men "talked" Black power he walked it. Ali had inoculated himself against racism. He had evolved. He was no longer the Black slave or Black sharecropper who cowered and showed fear when the KKK came to town. They didn't threaten him; he had become the "Threatener." Ali invented his own word (threatener) to fit the occasion.

All men must make this transition. As I said before, Black Americans are the only Americans not allowed to evolve. It is in the interest of very powerful people to keep Black Americans afraid, weak, and impotent. People hated Ali for the wrong reasons. He did not care. They called him, "nigger." He said, "I am the greatest." They threatened him. He knocked them out.

A reporter once told Pittsburg Steeler coach Mike Tomlin that his players liked him and thought he was doing a great job. Tomlin responded, "They need to be more concerned with what I think about them, because I don't give a damn what they think about me." I am no longer concerned about the racist: The racist needs to be concerned with me.

You think this is pride? This is trash talk? No, this is spiritual. My logic is supported by fact. Racism is demonic. Racism is evil. We give the devil power by fearing him. We must ignore, or better yet mock and laugh at racism and racist people.

St. Augustine wrote: *"The devil . . . the proud spirit cannot endure to be mocked."* Martin Luther wrote: *"The best way to drive out the devil, if he will not yield to text of scripture, is to jeer and flout him, for he cannot bear scorn."*

Most Black adults scream like schoolyard sissies whenever they see a confederate flag, blackface, or rebel statue. Instead of handling it man to man they run to their father, the government, demanding that a law be passed and that the person be punished for offending them.

A racist is a fool! A wise man does not argue with a fool. He will soon blow away with the dust. Black Americans remain at the bottom of every socioeconomic statistic because we spend too much of our time wrestling with racist fools who live in the mud. We should only concern ourselves with them if they attempt to do us or our loved ones physical harm. But most Blacks want to turn in their guns and prefer to leave that task to their daddy: the government.

An expanded version of Ralph Waldo Emerson's quote:

> What I must do is all that concerns me, not what the people think. This rule, equally arduous in actual and intellectual life, may serve for the whole distinction between greatness and meanness. It is the harder because you will always find those that think they know what is your duty better than you know it.

Blacks Americans are too concerned with what White Americans are doing or not doing. Because of this preoccupation Blacks cannot focus on what they "can" do. Jesus said it best when he said: "You hypocrite! First remove the beam out of your own eye then you can see clearly to remove the speck out of your brother's eye."

I don't have time to worry about how I am regarded by racists. They are fools! I should be concerned with how I am regarded by Christ. Racists should be more concerned with how I regard them.

I am the Threatener! I am the Storm! I invite you to join me.

KNOW THYSELF

Socrates said, "Man Know Thyself; It is the prerequisite knowledge." Sadly, for many Christian Americans their beliefs have become more and more arbitrary in regard to what it means to be a Christian or an

American. One might be able to have their own opinion when grappling with this subject, but when one combines their Christian beliefs with their Americanism, I believe the structure becomes clearer.

Where do you stand on the issues of the day? I have posed this question to many adults of every race and religion. Most of the time I find they usually do not know what those issues are. If they do know the issues, I am always surprised to find that few have taken the time to form an opinion. I am then illuminated to find that of the ones who have formed an opinion, most have turned to either emotion or tribalism, not their religion or facts, to guide them to their answer. Of those that call themselves religious, few apply these religious beliefs to their politics. And when proven wrong they hold to their erroneous view with a stiff-necked stubborn resistance. This explains pain inside of the Black community and why it is impossible to correct it by employing our present remedies.

Liberal Democrats are in the middle of a hundred-year plan to erase real Christianity from America and replace it with an apostate replica. So far they have succeeded beyond their wildest dreams. Consequently, these most important social issues that determine how we live are no longer governed by the entity that tells us how to live: GOD. As the Black preacher becomes more of an accomplice in this tragedy, the people, especially the young, are rudderless. They lack foundation, direction, or purpose. In this chapter we will discuss these issues, how the Iron Triangle is used to manipulate the masses, and where we should stand as Christians.

America's Descent

Alexander Tytler wrote in 1770 that Democratic nations of the past progressed through the following sequence:

1. From **bondage** to spiritual faith
2. From spiritual faith to great courage
3. From courage to liberty
4. From liberty to abundance

5. From abundance to selfishness
6. From selfishness to complacency
7. From complacency to apathy
8. From apathy to dependency
9. From dependency back to *bondage*

Any unbiased observer would conclude that America has descended from complacency and is now languishing in the age of apathy and teetering on the brink of dependency. Liberal politicians are consistently beating the drum of government health care, government education, government housing, government protection, government food, government transportation, government drug counseling, government-controlled retirement, etc. This apathetic mind-set has put this once-great nation on the road to bankruptcy.

Liberals have created a culture of death. Life expectancy has dropped in America for the third straight year since 2017 due mostly to suicide and drug overdoses. Suicides rose from 29,000 in 1999 to 47,000 in 2017, along with 72,000 overdose deaths in 2017. Furthermore, because of the liberal Democrat Party attacks on traditional families and values, according to the Center for Disease Control, the American birthrate has declined for the past 3 years. This is good news to democrats. Their policy to federally fund abortion has led to Nazi Party laws in America. These laws have corrupted the purpose of our federal government and put it in the business of murdering the citizens it was formed to protect on an industrial scale. Consequently, their assault on religion has created a society where the serving of the GOD who saves is being replaced by serving a government that destroys.

America is one election away from dependency. Dependency is the antithesis to freedom but is the "mothers' milk" to equality. Observe the effect it has had on the Black community in the ghettos, or more fittingly "Little Stalingrads." If you fancy the results there, you will love what they have in store for the rest of America.

Just as cancers and hurricanes are evil in themselves and are self-destructive, Liberalism is evil in itself and is eventually self-destructive.

Mark well the murder rate, abortion rate, drug abuse, vandalism, violence, ignorance, sloth, and disrespect for property that exists in the Black ghettos. These are the fruits of Liberalism.

Sadly, evil does exist in this world. Its aim is total destruction of its host even though it destroys itself in the process. Why? Man must have evil before it can recognize good. Evil is not random. It is well organized and has a strategy. One strategy is to "define deviancy down," to make Americans afraid to call it by its name. However, we can no longer afford to look evil in the face and smile while it destroys our children. Mark well Ephesians 6: 12 when it says: "*We wrestle not against flesh and blood but principalities, against powers, against spiritual darkness in this world, against spiritual wickedness in high places.*"

What other political party in history has had as its main priorities: the murder of infants, the death of religion, the destruction of the family, the spread of homosexuality, the perversion of children, and the exaltation of materialism? Only one: the LIBERAL. The Liberal requires that you have pride in your sin, even though our Bible tells us that Sodom was not destroyed for its sin but because of PRIDE in its sin.

In his book *Mere Christianity* C.S. Lewis called pride "the great sin." Lewis wrote:

According to Christian teachers, the essential vice, the utmost evil, is pride. Unchastity, anger, greed, drunkenness, and all that are mere fleabites in comparison; it was through pride that the devil became the devil. Pride leads to every other vice. It is the complete anti-God state of mind . . . But pride always means enmity—it *is* enmity. And not only enmity between man, but enmity to GOD. As long as you are proud you cannot know GOD . . . For Pride is a spiritual cancer; it eats up the very possibility of love or contentment, or even common sense . . . The real Black diabolical pride comes when you look down on others so much that you do not care what they think of you. Of course it is only right and often our duty not to care what people think of us, if we do so for the right reason namely, because we care so incomparably more what GOD thinks.

Christianity demands humility and repentance not pride. With pride there can be no repentance. Jesus said "you must be born again." Everyone that met Jesus was changed forever. Yet the prideful say "Jesus must accept me as I am. I will not change my lifestyle. I will not conform. I do not want his forgiveness because I have done nothing wrong. Jesus is wrong. I will not repent" Saul became Paul. Peter became Cephas. But the rich young ruler walked away sorrowfully. Liberalism and todays democrat party demand that you walk away. The disease of pride is creating a spiritual cancer and culminating in a lack of common sense that is turning America into Akrasia. Lewis defined Akrasia as a place where there is rationalization of evil, astate of mind in which someone acts against their better judgement through weakness of will. The gay pride parades and the wanton displays of violence, sexuality, and materialism in our culture are all representative of a society that has strayed away from the natural and spiritual order. We are in Akrasia.

An Iron Triangle has gripped the necks of America and is choking the life out of our nation. It has as its goal the complete transformation of American culture. What is American culture?

Webster's New Collegiate Dictionary defines culture as: "the integrated pattern of human behavior that includes thought, speech, action, and artifacts and depends upon man's capacity for learning and transmitting knowledge, to succeeding generations and the customary beliefs, social forms, and material traits of a racial, religious, or social group." Mores and values are defined as: "the fixed morally binding customs of a particular group." What are the customs, mores, and values of America and where did they come from?

One's morality must derive from an infallible source. I am a Christian. As a Christian I do not profess to have the right to judge, condemn, or convince fellow Christians. But I have a right and an obligation to inform them. My fellow Christians will then take the information and respond as they please. Even as imperfect as our nation's founding was, it is a fact that the Judeo-Christian ethic was the foundation on which our nation was built. Each brick that was mortared with secularism and human thought has been destroyed by the elements but those that survived the ravages of time were mortared by the Divine and evolved our country into a more perfect union The Declaration of Independence affirmed this ethic when it states, "We are endowed by our **creator** with certain unalienable rights." That Christian ethic steered us through wars against Fascism, Nazism, and Jim Crow, forcing America to add its national protections to members of the human family that GOD was already protecting and take those protections away from those that betrayed the Judeo-Christian ethic. Now America has decided again to add its national protections to those actions that go against the laws of nature, morality, history, and GOD.

Most Christians believe that the infallible source from which Christians derive our instruction is the WORD of GOD encapsulated in the Holy Bible. Christians believe that, as in the sport of boxing where everything "derives from the jab," everything in the life of a Christian should derive from our Christian theology, which should be contained in the Bible. We believe in the Ten Commandments and the teachings of Jesus Christ. On the foundation of those teachings we walk through this life unafraid and secure in the knowledge that we are saved by grace not by works. We are our brother's keeper and as iron sharpens iron, a friend sharpens his friend. That would mean that we do not judge. Judgment requires opinion through condemnation, which we have no authority to give. Nevertheless, it is not judgment to tell a man who is wearing blue pants that his pants are blue; that is a fact. However, it is judgment to tell a man in blue pants that his pants are ugly; that requires an opinion. But it is not judgment to tell a man wearing blue pants that wearing blue pants is against the law if that is a fact. Therefore, Christians are not allowed to give opinions or judgments but we are allowed to give facts, as long as these facts are based upon the infallible word of GOD. Following that line of thought, we Christians should speak the truth, in love, regarding the social issues of the day. We are obligated to do this because we believe that confession and repentance, not sinlessness, are absolutely essential to salvation. We must understand that when we sin it only begins the process that continues to confession, then repentance, and culminates in forgiveness. These ideas define us as Christians. Furthermore, we as Christians believe it is our duty and right to transfer our beliefs, our culture, and our way of life to our children. However, there are powerful forces in our midst that hate Christians and are trying their best to turn Christian children away from their religion and culture of their ancestors so that they must bow to governent. All educated men and women understand this. The Iron Triangle knows it. This why they must end religion.

History has recorded the destruction of nations that have attacked religion and warned nation states to avoid this folly. For this reason the founders placed "freedom of religion" first among guaranteed freedoms in our Bill of Rights. Government has been trying to take it away ever since. In his book "The Prince" a book many consider the political bible, Niccolo Michiavelli warned governments about the dangers of attacking religion. He wrote: "As the observance of religious rites is the foundation of a republic's greatness, so disrespect for them is the source of its ruin. Where fear of GOD is lacking, the state must either fail or be sustained by a fear of the ruler which may substitute for the lack of religion". Religion is failing in the Black community. The Iron Triangle with the Black Preacher at the helm is destroying it. Since GOD no longer controls our communities the ruler, in the body of the police, must.

Our culture and our children are at risk. The risk is difficult to defeat because we are continuously thwarted by an uncannily shrewd adversary that has used two of our greatest attributes against us. Those attributes are "tolerance" and "loyalty."

Do we Christians still believe our Bibles? If so, why do we allow ourselves and our children to be educated, represented, ministered to, and influenced by people who proudly profess an ideology that is completely counter to our belief system?

For example, in Matthew 5: 27-28, Jesus teaches against fornication and adultery and teaches that sex is only prescribed for married couples. In Mark 10: 6-9, Jesus described marriage as a union between a man and a woman when he said, "But at the beginning of creation God made them male and female. For this reason a man will leave his father and mother and be united to his wife, and the two will become one flesh. So they are no longer two but one." This is very plain but many Christians allow themselves to be led astray by Liberals that harp on the lie the Biblical prohibitions against homosexual behavior are only in the Old Testament and have no legitimacy today. However, logic dictates that homosexual behavior in the very least is fornication since people of the same sex, biblically, cannot be married. Remember, a man is to "leave his father and mother and cleave to his wife." Does this make the actions of gays and lesbians worse than those of sins committed by other Christians? I would say no. But the pride in their sin that drives their ambition to lead others and Christian children to accept and participate in homosexual activity should be particularly troubling to all Christian parents if they are to take the admonitions of Christ seriously. Yet many Christians vote knowingly and unknowingly for politicians who support these behaviors, send their children to schools that teach it, and ministers who either ignore or accept it in their churches. Why is this important? Jesus in Matthew 18: 5-6 speaks of terrible repercussions for adults that lead children astray. He said, "And whoever welcomes a little child like this in my name welcomes me. But if anyone causes one of these little ones who believe in me to sin, it would be better for him to have a large millstone hung around his neck and be drowned in the depths of the sea."

Through tolerance, we have allowed immorality to flow unchecked through our communities, schools, and churches, all under the misunderstood mantra "Judge not so you be not judged." Should we threaten, hurt, or cause harm to those we disagree with? No. But we are obligated to protect our children. It seems that the only time a person can be judged is when they speak the truth as it pertains to the scriptures. New York Senator Daniel Patrick Moynihan coined the term "defining deviance down" to describe the destruction of what we once believed as civilized normal behavior. The results of Christian tolerance have been catastrophic, as we will discuss later on.

It seems that the tumultuous sixties demoralized a large segment of the Christian community that still feels ashamed that they did not destroy the known wickedness and sinful behavior in their midst in the form of racism. Instead it had to be exposed and exploited by the then-outcast fringes of American society, which is now the Democratic Party base. The homosexuals, Communists, Socialists, and drug addicts exposed the sins of the Church, while many "good" Christians remained quiet, thus robbing them of much of their moral authority. But as the cunning serpent seduced the children of GOD in the garden and made them hide in shame, separating them from him, these children of darkness have so seduced Black Christians. But there is no condemnation in those that believe in Jesus Christ. GOD said that "he will take your sins and will remember them no more." To live in the condemnation of the sins of the past is to be defeated. The children of darkness have released their kin from the closet and have succeeded in shaming most Christians into the closet. But as Christ did before us, we must again place the serpent's head against our heel, admit our sins, ask his forgiveness, and thus reconcile ourselves with him and save our land. How do we do this?

We must go back to what we believe. Sadly, if one would ask Christians of most denominations what they believe they might get a long list of random answers. But what do Christians believe in regard to most controversial issues of our day? Moreover, how are our contradictions regarding these issues in our Christian talk versus our Christian walk not only destroying America but also our families and our very souls?

The following denominations and religions consider both homosexuality and abortion as sins and incompatible with the word of GOD. They include: Roman Catholics, Churches of Christ, Jehovah's Witnesses, Pentecostals, Baptists, Methodists, and Islam. Most Americans and the vast majority of African Americans consider themselves believers of one of these worldwide religions. However, their political affiliations do not reflect these values. Many of these Christians, especially Blacks, do not live their vote. Many are seduced by bribes in the form of social programs and government handouts to betray their religious faith and exclaim their support for these anti-religious groups by espousing their yearning for social justice.

However, there is nowhere in the Bible where caring for the poor and the indigent is the responsibility of the government. I am not saying that the government should not take care of those that can't take care of themselves, but I am suggesting that government should not take care of those that will not take of themselves. Our Holy Bible does say in II Thessalonians 3:10; "That if any would not work, neither should they eat." But more than that, it causes free men to become slaves. Christians, individually or collectively through the church, are given the responsibility for the poor. Government has taken over the role because too many churches have other priorities for their money (which we will discuss later). Consequently we are seeing the inevitable result of those that exchange their trust in GOD for trust in man. Where GOD frees, man enslaves. Where GOD gives, man takes. Where GOD sanctifies, man defiles.

Examine the lives of the ones that have taken the Liberals' offers. Go to their ghettos and crack houses and housing projects. You will find the vast majority of all of its inhabitants will proudly profess the doctrine of the Liberal Democratic Party. Jesus said, "What profits a man to gain the whole world and lose his soul?" Then examine the lives of those that have retained their faith and their beliefs.

Like Esau, America—and especially the Black community—has sold its birthright for a bowl of pottage. Many have traded the unlimited spiritual blessings of GOD for the empty existence and meager welfare check of the Liberal. We know better. Or do we? The school, pulpit, and politicians all regurgitate the same lie. We had a politician that ran for president of the United States of America exclaiming to the fearful that he was "HOPE" when our Bible clearly states in Psalms 42: 5: "Why art thou cast down, O my soul? And why art thou disquieted in me? Hope thou in GOD: for I shall yet praise him for the help of his countenance." Psalms 71:5 says: "For thou art my hope, O Lord GOD: thou art my trust from my youth." The First Commandment says: "Thou shalt have no other GOD before me."

Yet too many Western Christians have decided to choose other GODS. These GODS are men of flesh and bone who promise security and legitimacy in return for freedom. They preach a life of victimhood, hedonism, and no consequences. Yet there are always consequences. The prisons, cemeteries, and welfare rolls are filled with those that discovered this too late. Liberalism is the religion where these GODS are praised. How do we know this is true? Look around. Go to any ghetto or city plagued with crime, poverty, and promiscuity you will find this religion practiced. However, it is exponentially worse in communities where people profess Christianity but live, play, and vote as Liberals. The Black community is peculiar in this area. Not since the Biblical days of Moses and the children of Israel have a people been more blessed by GOD only to pursue other GODS and consequently cause the blessings of GOD to be suspended until they return to him.

Before 1965 most Black families could boast of never having a member go to prison, be addicted to drugs, divorced, chronically jobless, on welfare, a victim of a crime committed by a Black person, or reared in a fatherless home. By 1980, fifteen years after accepting Liberalism, it became strange not to find many of these maladies in the Black home.

How do we get back to our Father's praying ground? Our condition is not new. The past is prologue and those who do not learn from history are doomed to repeat it. After finishing the house of the Lord and being presented with a country prosperous and at peace, Solomon had a visit from GOD that constituted an opportunity and a warning. In II Chronicles 7:12-22 it is recorded:

> And the Lord appeared to Solomon by night, and said unto him, "I have heard thy prayer, and have chosen this place to myself for a house of sacrifice. If I shut up heaven that there be no rain, or if I command the locusts to devour the land, or if I send pestilence among my people; if my people, which are called by my name, shall humble themselves, and pray, and seek my face, and turn from their wicked ways; then will I hear from heaven, and will forgive their sin, and will heal their land . . . mine eyes and mine heart shall be there perpetually . . . and if thou wilt walk before me . . . and do according to all that I have commanded thee, and

shalt observe my statutes and my judgments; then will I establish the throne of thy kingdom . . . But if ye turn away and forsake my statutes and my commandments, which I have set before you . . . then will I pluck them up by the roots out of my land . . . and will make it to be a proverb and a byword among nations. And this house, which is high, shall be an astonishment to everyone that passeth by it; so that he shall say, "Why hath the LORD done thus unto this land, and unto this house?" And it shall be answered, *"Because they forsook the LORD GOD of their fathers which brought them out of Egypt, and laid hold on other gods, and worshipped them, and served them: therefore hath he brought all this evil upon them."*

Things are out of sync. They are out of order. Romans 10:14-15 asks: "How shall they hear without a preacher? And how shall they preach, except they be sent?" How indeed?

Section 3

—⁓—

THREE SIDES OF THE TRIANGLE

THE BLACK PREACHER: THE FIRST SIDE OF THE TRIANGLE

Near the end of World War II President Harry S. Truman was concerned about the invasion and occupation of the Japan. Although, the United States had dropped atomic bombs on the cities of Hiroshima and Nagasaki they still feared that the citizens of Japan would still fight to the death before they would allow any American to step foot on the Japanese mainland. Some war plans estimated that we would lose close to a million soldiers if the United States attempted such an invasion.

Earlier that year, the allies issued the Potsdam Declaration demanding the unconditional surrender of Japan. After two atomic bombs, the Japanese declared that they would surrender with one caveat: the Emperor Hirohito must remain Sovereign Ruler of Japan. Many of the American hardliners scoffed, demanding that the Potsdam Declaration had to be adhered to and that Japan was in no position to make any demands. But Harry Truman recognized an opportunity.

He understood that the Japanese people saw the Emperor as a GODlike figure and would do whatever he commanded. Truman understood. If he controlled who the Japanese people perceived to be God's messenger, he could control Japan. Truman accepted the terms, took control of Hirohito, and the United States Armed Forces walked into Japan without firing a shot. They have had a peaceful existence there since 1945.

Like the story of occupied Japan, the untold story of Black degradation in America is the story of control. Like Harry Truman in Japan; the slave master, the Southern politician, and the Liberal discovered early where lay the "critical mass" of the people they wanted to subjugate: it wrested in the person of the Black preacher. Control GOD'S messenger and you control the people.

THE PIMP

Son I bought you up in the Church and to respect men of GOD.
Now I'm gonna tell you something that's gonna hurt me to tell.
You trust a bootlegger before you trust most Black preachers.

—Ivory Ellison

In this chapter I will illustrate eight points:

1. The Black church was created by racist Whites and is now maintained mostly but not completely by sellout apostate Black preachers.
2. Black church controlled by the Black preacher was created by White plantation owners, the ancestors of today's Democratic Party, more as a vehicle to control their Black slaves and later the Black population as opposed to evangelizing to them.
3. The vast majority of Black preachers are descendants of an apostate order whose primary purpose is to serve the White Liberal Democratic Party power and enrich themselves. They do this by espousing blasphemous doctrines of which the Prosperity Gospel and Black Liberation Theology are just two of many.

4. The apostate Black clergy and their adulterous relationship with the Democratic Party has contaminated the Church, the Black community, and this nation by fomenting pride, division, unforgiveness, and conflict.

5. You will come away with a better understanding of the tactics used by the Democratic Party to employ their almost universal support in the Black church as leverage to coerce a guilt-ridden White America into passing Socialist, anti-Christian policies that are hurting America and destroying the Black community.

6. The Black preacher's almost absolute loyalty to the Liberal Democratic Party has rendered the Black church almost ineffective in its "stated" goal of saving souls for Christ and has turned it into a walking contradiction, where its anti-Christian political stance negates its ecclesiastical obligations. How can they preach the schizophrenic concept that a man is a child of GOD and a victim? It is a lie. And they still tell it daily.

7. The Black preacher is one of the most corrupt professions in America and the American Christian Church again holds the key to saving not just Black America but all of America.

8. The "Black church" is an oxymoron. There isn't any "Black church," "White church," or "Red church." There is only ONE CHURCH: the one set up by Jesus Christ.

THE BEGINNING

In the classic masterpiece *Mere Christianity,* C.S. Lewis wrote the following concerning preachers and the Church's involvement in politics:

People say the "The Church ought to give us lead." That is true if they mean it in the **right way, but false if they mean it in the wrong way** . . . But, of course, when they ask for a lead from the Church most people mean they want the clergy to put out a political program. That is silly. The clergy are those particular people within the whole Church who have been specially trained and set aside to look after what concerns us as creatures who are going to live forever: and we are asking them to do a quite different job for which they have not been trained. The job is really on us, on the laymen. The application of Christian principles, say to trade unionism or education, must come from the Christian trade unionists and Christian schoolmasters: just as Christian literature comes from Christian novelists and dramatists—not from the bench of bishops getting together and trying to write plays and novels in their spare time.

The Democratic Party controls most Black preachers. The Black preacher controls the Black church. And the Black church is the spout that pours the Black community into the Democratic Party. A Church being a proxy for a political party is bad enough, but when a Church is a proxy to a party that is diametrically opposed to almost everything it is supposed to believe it is guilty of blasphemy. The old Mafia saying, "A fish rots from the head down," explains why the Black community is in such trouble. The Black church is the head of the Black community, and in most cases its head. It has abandoned its original calling to prepare man for eternal life and has turned to the earthly lure of politics. Most Black preachers are apostate. How did this happen? Taylor Branch wrote:

> The Negro church, legal in some respects before the Negro family, became more solvent than the undertaker . . . For the next century, a man with a burning desire to be a saint might well find himself competing with another preacher intent only on making a fortune, as all roads converged at the Negro church.

The Black preacher, from his marginalized position in slavery, was always an easy mark for any White person, especially Liberals. For example, according to Blackgenocide.org when Margaret Sanger, a believer in eugenics, abortion rights, and the founder of Planned Parenthood, started a project designed to exterminate the Black community called "Negro Project" in 1939, the most important part of her plan was to use

Black ministers as proxies to spread her message throughout the community. They were willing—and most of the time paid—participants. And knowingly or unknowingly were complicit in the greatest fratricidal event in world history.

Nevertheless, betraying your community and your oath to GOD is not strange for the office of Black minister; in most cases it is part of the job description. Ironically the only people who do not know this are the "loyal" Christian Democrat Black Americans. Evil people will always find a way to turn your strengths into weaknesses. Loyalty is strength; the Black Democrat preacher has turned it into a suicide vest. It has always been thus.

In 1938 the Carnegie Foundation, for the advancement of teaching, hired Swedish Nobel-Laureate economist Gunner Myrdal to author a study on race relations in America. It concluded in the book *An American Dilemma: The Negro Problem in America*. This book was cited in Brown vs. Board of Education and laid the ground work for Affirmative Action and racial integration. Regarding the founding and the character of the Negro church, Myrdal wrote:

> With few exceptions the Negro slaves brought to America had not been converted to Christianity. For nearly a century many slave holders felt reluctant to let the Negro slaves receive religious instruction as there was a belief that a baptized Christian could not be held as a slave. But when theologians, legislatures, and courts declared around the year 1700, that conversion to Christianity was not incompatible with the worldly status of a slave, slaveholders went out of their way to provide a religious teaching and a place for worship for their slaves, or at least did nothing to hinder missionary work among them. Their primary motive undoubtedly was that the Christian religion, as it was expounded, suited their interests in keeping the slaves humble, meek, and obedient...**Undoubtedly the great bulk of Southern Negro preachers advocated complete acceptance of slave status**... when they could see one of their own number, the preacher, rise above the level of slave hood and even occasionally be admired by

White people. The slaves on a plantation could regard the Negro preacher as their leader—one who could go to the White master and beg for trivial favors.

He went on to say:

In practically all rural areas, and in many of the urban ones, the preacher stood out as the acknowledged local leader of the Negros. His function became to transmit the Whites' wishes to the Negroes and to beg the Whites for favors for his people. He became—in our terminology—the typical accommodating Negro leader. **To this degree the Negro Church perpetuated the traditions of slavery.**

About his morals:

In accordance with Baptist and Methodist tenets, he preaches puritanical morals, and yet is often far from exemplary in his own life and sometimes has connections with the underworld. These paradoxes exist, as DuBois puts it, the Negro preacher is "a leader, a politician, an orator a 'boss,' an intriguer, an idealist."

Black comedians have made millions satirizing flamboyant and hypocritical Black clergy. The press enjoys writing about their relationships with organized crime, Black street gangs, money laundering, drugs, extravagant vanity, and women other than their wives. Nevertheless, the blind loyalty of Black Democrat Christians makes them immune.

Since I am a sinner, it is not my job to record the sins of other men. Nevertheless, it is my duty to bring your attention to organized crime and hypocrisy. Politically, most Black preachers have been an employee for the Democratic Party since its inception in 1800. He does not care where the party stands on issues or who or what the politicians stand for. The Democrats are and will forever be his master and he must bring his master the votes.

Myrdal wrote:

Where Negroes vote, preachers frequently take a stand and use their influence and their pulpit to swing Negro votes. Although the feeling is prevalent among Negroes as among Whites, that clergymen should have nothing to do with politics, the Negro preacher's position as community leader, as well as his desire to get money for his church and even for himself, often leads him to have some sort of tie with a political machine or candidate.

St. Jerome stated, "avoid like the plague the man that fancies himself a clergyman and a businessman." Politics is business. Consequently, many of our ministers have found ways to make money outside of the pulpit. Christ's statement that "you cannot serve both GOD and mammon" is proven in the body of most Black preachers. He seems to always find himself in something profitable but nefarious for his people then and now.

It was recently exposed by the *Washington Post* on June 12, 2012, how the greed of Black preachers helped fuel the greatest financial crisis in world history. Elizabeth Jacobson, a former loan officer at Wells Fargo Bank, testified in federal court that Wells Fargo gave Black preachers a percentage of their profits if they opened their churches to them and allowed them to push subprime loans to their members. Consequently, most of the loans were bad and many church members lost their homes but the preachers got rich and America went into the Great Recession.

They even engaged in usury and legalized loansharking to the Black community in the practice of payday lending. According to the Federal Consumer Financial Protection Bureau, a typical payday lender charges an APR of 400 percent compared to a credit card, which is between 12 percent to 30 percent. Also because you write a post-dated check for collateral, payday lenders will have you arrested if you miss one payment. It has been reported that between 25 percent and 30 percent of the borrowers are Black. These companies are predatory and are the modern equivalent of a mafia loan shark. So, it would make sense that on June 7,

2018, the front page of the *Washington Post* read: "Payday Lenders turn to Churches." The article reads:

> The Federal Consumer Financial Protection Bureau has spent years developing industry regulations addressing concerns that borrowers were being trapped in debt. In response some **payday lenders** have sought to build support for their business by forging relationships with **Black churches**. Black churches have a long history of helping congregations find financial footing historians say. . . . In Ohio, the Cleveland Clergy Coalition, registered as a nonprofit last year, has submitted testimony in favor of payday lending to a committee considering a bill to tighten restrictions on the industry and showed up at legislative hearings with T-shirts saying "Protect Access To Credit." Aaron Philips, a pastor and the group's executive director said . . . he could not divulge whether donations were made to his group from lenders. "The group is supporting the lenders," he said "because it's best for our community, not because we have any financial support from them."

These tragedies are only a few examples of how the Black preacher has always evolved to feed his greed. The marriage of politics, money, and religion reaffirms the genius behind the doctrine of the separation of church and state. It is a concept of great controversy. It seems, however, that it is necessary and retains serious weight and merit when its negative effects on history are weighed against its positive impacts. This is because politics will taint almost everything it touches—especially religion. One would think religious guidance would have a positive effect on government. However, when flawed men and women that are drawn to political power they can use the mysticism of religion to control the man-made power of government. There is much room for mischief and they very seldom refrain from indulging. Enough space does not exist to provide examples of the damage this partnership has caused in history but here are a few examples: The Sanhedrin used this power to crucify Christ. The Puritans during the

Salem Witch Trials used it to hang and burn innocent people accused of witchcraft. The Catholics used it during the Inquisition to burn people they considered heretics. The "religious holy man" Gregori Rasputin used it to destroy the Romanov dynasty in Russia.

The flaw here does not rest in the fact that politicians will attempt to leverage the influence of the Church to ascertain power. It is well known that throughout history the term "politician" has been associated with sleight of hand and sharp dealing. The love, peace, and charity of the Church were the counterweight that always balanced the war, betrayal, and harshness of politics. But, whenever these two worlds become partners the natural order of the society is disjointed. When preachers become politicians they become more concerned with the affairs of men rather than the affairs of GOD. Moreover, the Church, in its purist form, always has the ability to bend politics to its will. The true disciples of Christ, starting with the original twelve, were never influenced by politics; politics were influenced by them and Rome fell.

True men of GOD do not need to waddle in the mud of politics. They answer to a higher power. A minister engaging in the world of politics to gain power and influence is equivalent to a married man engaging with a prostitute for companionship. Picture a surgeon in the middle of a heart transplant being interrupted to march against a politician in blackface. He wouldn't consider it. A doctor saves lives. A minister saves lives and souls. Ministers speaking to their congregation and resting their message on the true word of GOD have changed the course of nations. He didn't do this by taking handouts and cash from politicians but by releasing a well-informed, spiritually anchored citizenry into the community who, in return, demand their local politics reflect their values.

Ministers should lead from the scriptures, never from the law. They should speak from the pulpit not from the halls of government. They, as individuals, should have no voice in government; their congregations should be their voices. Why do we never see Supreme Court justices or federal judges endorsing, campaigning for, or receiving cash handouts from politicians? They understand that their credibility rests on their ability to appear unbiased in the eyes of the public.

America speaks loudly and authoritatively in regard to the concept of the separation of church and state. But they would scream from the highest mountain if they understood that there should be a higher and thicker wall between education and state. There should be a wall of separation that protects religion and education from the sultry world of politics. Politics has the tendency to contaminate almost everything it touches. Through education it contaminates children and through the Church it contaminates the word of GOD. In the Black community this whole process is backward and has precipitated the very same cultural vortex that has occurred throughout history when these two extremes meet.

The Founding Fathers, understanding the nature of this dynamic, marked our Constitution so that these mistakes would not be realized in America. However, the forever-marginalized Black preacher whose influence reached only as far as his congregation migrated was ripe for manipulation. For decades Liberals sought a way to leverage the Black community's influence toward their Godless causes. For many years they were unsuccessful but through the civil rights movement and Black leadership's hunger for integration, Liberals convinced Black preachers to commit a fatal sin. This sin was offered to Jesus but he would not bow. This is how it was described in Matthew 4: 8-10:

> *Again, the devil taketh him up into an exceeding high mountain, and sheweth him all the kingdoms of the world, and the glory of them; And saith unto him, All these things will I give thee, if thou wilt fall down and worship me. Then saith Jesus unto him, Get thee hence, Satan: for it is written, thou shalt worship the Lord thy God and him only shalt thou serve.*

Too many Black preachers have agreed to bow down and worship him. If you doubt me look at the condition of their flock.

Wikipedia defines "poverty pimp" as a sarcastic label:

Used to convey the opinion that an individual or group is benefiting unduly by acting as an intermediary on behalf of the poor, the disadvantaged, or some other "victimized" group. Those who use this appellation suggest that those so labeled profit unduly from the misfortune of others, and therefore do not really wish the societal problems that they appear to work on so assiduously be eliminated permanently, as it is not in their own interest for this to happen. The most frequent targets of this accusation are those receiving government funding or soliciting private charity to work on issues on behalf of various disadvantaged individuals or groups, but who never seem to be able to show any amelioration of the problems experienced by their target population.

Some even suggest that that if profit was eliminated as a factor, greater steps in the alleviation of the oppressive situations could begin to truly occur. Thus religious leaders involved in politics have forgotten religion.

It is a wicked irony that Liberals are using Black religious figures to destroy religion among Black people. It was always understood by Liberals that the eradication of religion was necessary to usher in the society they coveted. They excel in the field of psychiatry and believe religion is backward, superstitious, and stupid. They swore to stamp it out. Many of their mainstream modern heroes, including Sigmund Freud, Wilhelm Wundt, Dr. Brock Chisholm, and many others were the founders of this new-wave idea of changing American society through the eradicating of religion. Freud wrote in "Future of Illusions:

(Religious ideas) which profess to be dogmas . . . are not the residue of experience or the final result of reflection. They are illusions, fulfillments of the oldest, strongest, and most insistent wishes of mankind; the secret of their strength is the strength of these wishes.

My Eyes Are Opened

Before my first foray into politics I went to my father for advice. After advising me on many areas he ended his advice with a statement. He said, "Son, trust a bootlegger before you trust most Black preachers." It made such a lasting impression on me because it was anathema to everything I had been previously been taught. My father brought us up in the Church. As a matter of fact, we were so into the Church that at the age of nine my father taught me and three of my siblings to play instruments and sing in three-part harmony and then drafted us into a singing group called The Ellison Family. We made three albums, an assortment of records, and toured the whole South, part of the Midwest, and the East Coast singing good, down-home gospel music. About 98 percent of the venues we played were Black churches and my father knew all of the preachers personally. His knowledge was increased by the fact that he was the host of a six hour radio program that aired five days a week that played nothing but Black gospel music and serviced the Black church.

For over twenty-five years he never spoke disparagingly about the institution until that night. One caveat: he made me understand that there were still some good preachers out there but they were in the very slim minority. He backed up his admonition with information that will remain private between us but I found very soon that the half had not been told. Their treachery ran deeper than I could ever imagine. There is a common saying in the Black community: most "Black preachers talk Black, live White, and think green." I was going to find that it was more than a saying.

After returning to South Carolina I decided to seek political support in my run for Congress. I examined the record of my opponent Jim Clyburn and understanding where he stood on the issues versus where I and the Black church "officially" stood. I was pretty convinced I could garner some support, my father's admonition notwithstanding. The Baptist, Methodist, AME, CME Church of GOD in Christ, Catholic Church, etc. all agreed with me on abortion, gay rights, school choice, church and state, the work ethic, and the death penalty and they disagreed with my opponent. Nevertheless, I found that they were motivated more by man's money than GOD'S law. After meeting with many ministers, showing them the data on my opponent, my positions, and how they conferred with the concepts of their Church affiliation, I was usually confronted with the same question: how much are you willing to pay me for my services and the votes of my congregation? It was done so matter-of-fact, like a cashier giving you the sum total of the goods you bought at the grocery store, that I knew this had been going on for some time. This had to be tradition.

Nowhere in the world is religion more politicized than the Black community and the Middle East. And in both places the powerful use their constituents' as suicide bombers. My opponent had probably paid most of the Black Preachers with money from the DNC. If I was willing to pay more they would come to me. The starting rate was ten dollars per vote. It was all legal. In political terms it was called "street money." C.S. Lewis stated: "All mortals tend to turn into the thing they pretend to be." Many of these men choose to don the attire and the vocation of a pimp. Most have stopped pretending. Instead of pimping flesh they now pimp the future of their people. I refused to participate in the buying. If the preacher was the pimp, the politician had to be the John. I refused to be a John. After lamenting about my ability to collect with the Black masses, a Black Democrat told me, "You're not offering to give them anything." I responded, "Like welfare." He said yes. I responded, "It's killing the Black family; I can't offer to expand that." He said, "Son, that doesn't matter. A nigger will drink a liquid with poison written on it, if it's free." He was pointing out a fact. The Iron Triangle knows it is peddling poison to the Black community. And like a drug addict pursuing the drug pusher, most in the Black community and the Democratic Party understand the relationship. They know it's poison, but like the hopeless addict, filled with fear and racked with pain, most Blacks knowingly drink the poison. The Iron Triangle is the beneficiary.

"Souls to the Polls"

If there was any doubt that the Black preacher and Black civic organizer was in complete control of the Liberal Democratic Party, I give you "Souls to the Polls." This evidence is the payoff. It's the smoking gun. It's the Rodney King tape of Liberal Democrats and Iron Triangle collusion. They used to lie about it. They at least used to deny it. But like mobster John Gotti, they have now become so arrogant they flaunt their contempt for the world to see. Because they have calculated that the Black community will not care. They've surmised: if gay marriage, partial-birth abortion, transgender support, outlawing prayer, and passing out free birth control to children did not run Black Christians away, nothing will. They might be right. But I believe enough will care to make a difference.

The November 4, 2018, edition of the *Orlando Sentinel* reported on an annual tradition in the Black churches called "Souls to the Polls." It's a day when sellout Black preachers, Black civic organizations, the Democratic Party, and Godless Liberals set aside all pretense and converge in an arrogant and wanton display of their adultery in plain view, just as Absalom did, on the palace roof, with the wives of his father, King David. To quote the *Sentinel*:

> Overall, African Americans—13.3 percent of the electorate— make up 17 percent of early voters going into Sunday, the traditional "Souls to the Polls" day when buses take large groups directly from churches to early voting sites. Democratic gubernatorial candidate Andrew Gillum joined one such event in Miami Sunday.

"Souls to the Polls" is a Black national tradition and a Black national disgrace. It displays open contempt toward Jesus Christ, His Church, America, and the Black community. It is the continual nationwide exploitation of Black Americans and celebrates the prostitution of the Church by the same Democratic Party that has exploited them since 1800. There's a "Soul to the Polls" organization in Milwaukee, North

Carolina, Georgia, and where ever there is a significant number of Black people.

" 'Souls to the Polls' is really a historic day for the Black church," said Rhonda Thomas, the pastor at New Generation Baptist Church in Opa-Locka, Florida. "We feel like if anyone could move people, it would be the clergy." The Rev. Raymond Bishop, pastor of Mount Pilgrim Baptist Church, is one of the most active practitioners of "Souls to the Polls." He said, "It is something most African American churches have done forever without having a particular title to it." Oh, there was a title for it. They called it "street money" and "bribery." Believe me, no Black preacher is doing this for free.

"Souls to the Polls" would be bad enough if Black parishioners were supporting politicians and political policy that supported their ecclesiastical and religious values. But the fact that the people who organize "Souls to the Polls" and the party that benefit from 90 percent of the vote on that day stand in direct opposition to most important aspects of Christianity and are actually working to make it illegal in America has a wicked irony. Follow the money. You will discover that the people who organize and fund this treachery support abortion up to the ninth month and open borders. They are atheist, Communists, and anarchists. They support every sort of evil and they control the Iron Triangle.

"Souls to the Polls" is sponsored by an organization called PICO National Network. PICO supports among other things . . . wait for it . . . full citizenship rights for immigrants who are in the United States illegally and universal health care. PICO receives money from the Open Society Foundation. Its founder is George Soros. Soros's Open Society Foundation supports, among other things, the human rights of prostitutes, drug users, LGBTQ, and illegal immigrants. They also receive a large amount of their money from the Democracy Alliance. The president of the Democracy Alliance is Gara LaMarche. LaMarche is a long-time Progressive activist and close ally of George Soros.

These people care nothing about the Black community. The only interest Southern Democrats had in Black Americans was their ability to pick cotton. The only interest George Soros has in the Black community is the Black vote and its ability to put him and the Democratic Party in control of the United States government and the world. Most Black Americans are still pawns being exploited in a chess match played by masters. They use the false incentive that they can make the former slaves equal to this master by promising them that he will tackle income inequality, give them free health care, and impart social justice. It's the same lie they've been telling for sixty years. Why change it? It seems to always work. Some say Black Americans deserve what they get.

The November 2013 edition of *Esquire Magazine* carried a piece called, "The New Ideological Spectrum." In it they named a section of this spectrum "The Gospel Left." They are described as, "Party-line Progressives (Liberals) every day except Sunday." In other words, they are the "American hypocrites." It makes up 11 percent of the American electorate. It consists mostly of African Americans and females. They are less educated and have lower incomes than most other segments and are very religious. Though a majority favor restrictions on gay marriage, they tend to be pro-life a pro-Second Amendment policy, and are strongly pro-school choice and pro-family. They believe two lies: government plays a vital role in social justice and tackling inequality. Obama, the Democrat won 99 percent of that vote in 2008 and 95 percent in 2012. Clinton won 90 percent in 2016.

What happened to the Jesus example? I have lived long enough to understand that one cannot trade material possessions for peace. Those that do not understand this are not worthy to lead a people in a religious society. Vanity and Christianity are irreconcilable.

And vanity in the Christian ministry leads to the destruction of a people. Vanity leads men to deeds that fill the hunger of their vanity. When one strikes out against evil, the forces of evil will use the threat of destroying these possessions in an effort to check your behavior, or the incentive of adding to these possessions in an effort to invest in your whoredom. Today's Black religious environment is mostly consumed with the latter. For those who are blind and disagree, I present the condition of the majority of Black America as evidence to their crimes. The lie that government can eradicate inequality and provide social justice is a terrible heresy.

"Street Cred.": Million Man March Award

Million Man March October 16, 1996

With President and Mrs. Bush, 2002

With daughter Skyy and South Carolina Senator Lindsay Graham

With icon of freedom James Meredith

With Oklahoma Congressman JC Watts

With NY Mayor Rudy Guiliani

With SC Congressman Bob Inglis (center)

President Gerald Ford and Father-In-Law, Dr. John C. Calhoun, Special Assistant to the President in the Oval Office

Ellison Family Gospel Singers, 1978
(From left to right: Vince, Virginia, Father Ivory, Jonathan,
Mother Ella, Renatha, Ira, Sylvia, Marvin)

Vince with his brothers at their home church in Jackson, TN (from left to right)
Jonathan, Robert and Marvin

Jonathan (brother), Ivory (Father), Ruben (brother-in-law), Marvin (brother), Timothy (brother-in-law) and Vince

Father and Mother In-Law, Dr. John and Mrs. Chorsie Calhoun at the White House

Blacks Not At Home In Democrat Party

By Vince Ellison

Ellison Pushes Conservative Values For 6th District

By David J. Owens

Democratic Party doesn't reflect values of African-Americans

African-Americans must become competitive in U.S. marketplace

The educational, economic and moral development of our people must be retrieved from the government and given back to the people. When the people have been empowered and constitutionally protected by the government, they have always excelled.

Black leaders fear kids won't achieve

Success comes from hard work, not affirmative action programs

Election-year racial politics an absurd parade

At home "The Sanctuary" in the Blue Ridge Mountains of Virginia

Communism, Marxism Infiltrate the "Black" Church

Black Liberation Theology is a heresy that has polluted the "Black" Church since that the early 1970s. Because of its rabid racism, this ideology has made it impossible for White and Black Christians to reconcile.

Consequently, for the past forty years the Church has been powerless to turn back the assault that is being led against it by Liberals in the Democratic Party. According to Dr. C. Eric Lincoln and Lawrence H. Mamiya, in 1990 over one-third of Black clergy have been influenced by this heresy. I'm sure now there are many more.

In many ways the hatred caused by their racism has led many of the Churches that espouse Black Liberation Theology to side with the satanic forces in the Democratic Party. These forces will eventually lead to their destruction and the destruction of the Church as a whole if they are not stopped. Evidence suggests Black Liberation Theology is a Marxist/Communist plan within the Democratic Party to sabotage reconciliation and foment division among Black and White Christians. A unified Christian community is the death knell to Liberalism in the Democratic Party. Many Black preachers are greedy, ignorant pawns in a not-so-secret global war and are leading their congregations to the Marxist/Communist elements in the Democratic Party. How do I know this is true? They wrote it all down!

After Malcolm X's proclamation against Christianity in the 1950s, calling it a White man's religion, Dr. James Cone and fifty-one concerned clergy calling themselves the National Committee of Negro Churchmen bought a full-page ad in the *New York Times* to publish their Black Power statement. They called this theology Black Liberation Theology and wrote several books on it. Black religion expert James Walton said, "James Cone believed the New Testament revealed Jesus as one who identified with those suffering under oppression, the socially marginalized, and the cultural outcasts . . . Therefore Jesus reveals himself as Black in order to disrupt and dismantle White oppression."

Again Black leaders are not telling the Black community that they are free, dynamic, blessed, and undefeatable but telling them that they are oppressed, socially marginalized, and outcasts. If your leaders think this about you what do they expect of you?

Dwight Hopkins, a professor of Divinity at the University of Chicago, said, "Jesus says my mission is to eradicate poverty and to bring about freedom and liberation for the oppressed." The main concept of Black Liberation Theology proclaims that Black Americans are not free. Blacks live in a world governed by racism and White supremacy. It proclaims that they are oppressed. They are victims. They are unwanted and despised, just as Jesus was. Jesus therefore would side with the oppressed (Black people) not the oppressor (White people). They believed this oppression and poverty could only be alleviated through government control or Marxism.

Anthony B. Bradley PhD describes it like this: "In Cone's view, Whites consider Blacks animals, outside the realm of humanity, and attempted to destroy Black identity through racial assimilation and integration programs—as if Blacks have no legitimate existence apart from whiteness. Black theology is the theological expression of people deprived of social and political power." In *For My People: Black Theology and the Black Church,* Cone explains, "The Christian faith does not possess in its nature the means for analyzing the structure of capitalism. Marxism as a tool of social analysis can disclose the gap between appearance and reality, and thereby help Christians to see how things really are."

Another advocate of Black Liberation Theology is Harvard-educated and Harvard Professor Cornel West. In the book *Prophesy Deliverance*, West believes that Marxists and Black theologians should work together for social change and for those who are victims of oppression. Economic parity and redistribution of wealth are cornerstones of Marxism and Black Liberation Theology. This is not controversial. Cornel West is honest. He openly admits it. Clarence Shole' Johnson wrote in the essay, "Cornel West, African America Critical Thought, and the Quest for Social Justice":

The aim of African American critical thought therefore is to liberate Blacks from this oppressive existential situation but more so from the contemporary society that nurtures and sustains it. It is his hope that these efforts will result in the formation of an alliance between prophetic Christianity and Progressive Marxist social thought.

West also openly admits that the primary avenue for this indoctrination is the Black church. Many others agree with him. President Barack Obama's pastor Jeremiah Wright preaches Black Liberation Theology. An essay written for the Institute for Democratic Socialism called "The Black church and Marxism: What Do They Have to Say to Each Other" was written back in 1980. This partnership has been developing in plain sight for the last five decades yet most Black churchgoers do not even know it exists or that they have been indoctrinated in it without their knowledge.

During a July 2018 appearance on Tucker Carlson Tonight, on the Fox News Channel, Dr. West, while justifying his Marxist/ Socialist views and those of most Democrats, happily revealed that Rev. Dr. Martin Luther King Jr. was a Democratic Socialist. This explains the absolute salacious slander Dr. King committed in the now famous "I have a Dream" speech when he cemented in the psyche of Black America, the United States, and the world, this LIE: "The Negro is still not free." I was one of those Negroes to whom he was referring. But Jesus Christ said he made me free! He said I was born free! I affirm my freedom! No one can take it away! I defy anyone to try! Who are these liars to tell me any different. Should we follow man or GOD?

In addition to that, I do not ask anyone or anything for my freedom. I just "AM." If you own a car, do you ask someone before you drive it? If you do, by default you are acknowledging that they are the true owner, not you. It is the same with your freedom. Once you ask someone for it, you have admitted by default that they own your freedom and you are a slave. I am a free man: I cannot be oppressed. I am a free man: I do not care if someone despises me. I still love them. I am a free man: I cannot be cast out because I do not covet the company of those that do not covet mine. Therefore, I have no need for Black Liberation Theology.

Why is this partnership between Marxism and the "Black" Church problematic? One reason is because one of the tenets of Marxism is athe-ism! Yes, you read correctly. Many Black preachers have partnered with an ideology that believes that GOD needs to be eradicated from the face of the Earth! The insanity of this stance cannot be overstated. It's like Jews siding with Hitler. But, we did have Black slaves fighting for the Confederacy.

In his work *A Contribution to the Critique of Hegel's Philosophy of Right*, Karl Marx, the founder of Marxism, said of religion: "It is the opium of the people. The abolition of religion as the illusory happiness of the people is the demand for their real happiness."

The Marxist atheism comes from a belief that their fundamental strength must come from their own objective power as opposed to other sources (intellectuals, GOD, etc.). Under Marxist/Communist doctrine, religion retarded human development and outlawing it became a state practice. In his book *Religion*, Vladimir Lenin said: "Atheism is a natural and inseparable part of Marxism, of the theory and practice of scientific Socialism."

Marxism is slavery on steroids. A very small group of the majority controls all means of production and distribution. They control war and peace. They control who gets rich and who remains poor. They eradicate all institutions including the family, universities, schools, private prop-erty, etc. Then they usually take the members of the minority class and exterminate them all.

Why then would the Black preachers choose to collude with a politi-cal movement that wants to eradicate the Church? They've been part of one for the past fifty years anyway. If it doesn't matter to them that the Democrats support abortion, LGBTQ lifestyle, and the destruction of the family, why would it bother them that this same party supports athe-ism and the destruction of the Church? They are just evil traitors and cannot see past the money they are being paid by their handlers in the Democratic Party. Pimps, drug dealers, and assassins possess the same spirit.

This is happening in real time. The Black preachers helped the Liberal Democrats attain power. Now the Liberal Democrats are dismantling religion. Black preacher support is outlawing prayer in schools and outlawing the displaying of the Ten Commandments in public. The Democrats demanded that nuns provide birth control, boy scouts allow gay scout leaders, Catholic Charities can no longer function in Washington, DC, because they won't allow gay adoption, and Obamacare allows for free transsexual operations and abortions on demand.

The Spirit of Esau has consumed many of the members of this congregation and made them the antithesis of what GOD intended.

What is the Spirit of Esau? It is the spirit of hatred, victimization, and revenge that Esau felt against his brother Jacob who had wronged him. This spirit causes separation from GOD, your brothers and sisters in Christ, and will eventually lead to your own destruction. Like Esau many Black Americas have sold their birthright (vote, freedom, family, etc.) for a bowl of pottage (government handout, racism, envy, etc.) and are now angry at the results. They find scapegoats for their failures. Esau had Jacob. Blacks have White racism. Because of these destructive spirits both have remained subservient in their own land.

Black Liberation Theology is illogical. It teaches Black people that America is a society polluted with White racism. It contends that White people see Blacks as animals. It teaches that Whites hate Blacks and seek their destruction. What would Black deliverance look like? Destroy American democracy and capitalism where we have seen some Black people reach the zenith of power and wealth and replace it with Marxism. Marxism is a system where the worst White people will have absolute power, with no checks and balances and absolute control of everything you do and say.

How is this better for Black people? It isn't. It is good for the Marxist Black preacher, the Marxist Black politicians, and the Marxist Black civic leaders. It's good for the Iron Triangle only.

These Black preachers don't believe their own ideology. One of the tenets of Marxism is that the leaders live and struggle with the proletariat (the poor). Instead, most of these so-called Marxists are part of the bourgeoisie (the upper part of the middle class). They swim in counter-revolutionary activity. They sell their books for profit. They live in large houses far away for the poor. They drive large expensive cars. The fruits of their labor are death to their people.

In the movie *The Hunchback of Notre Dame*, the evil and sadistic priest, Judge Claude Frollo keeps the hunchback Quasimodo under his control by having Quasimodo recite terrible things about himself. Frollo says, "You are ugly." Quasimodo says, "I am ugly." Frollo says, "You are deformed." Quasimodo says, "I am deformed." He is told by Frollo that the world will hate him and that Frollo is his only friend and protector, which is something Quasimodo believes.

In the movie *Glory*, one of the Black Union soldiers exclaimed, "It seems like the whole world hates the nigger." The Iron Triangle screams this message to Black America and the world every day. It has had a devastating effect. It has enslaved the minds of a majority of the Black community. The free mind aspires. The slave mind cannot. The free mind hopes. The mind that has accepted its slavery cannot. The music of the current hip-hop culture testifies to the anger, hopelessness, and fear of the slave mind, the coarse language, the diffused attire, the rejection of all beauty and grace, the celebration of the vile, grotesque, and the obnoxious. This is the generation that believes the pronouncements of its Black leaders: You are unwanted. You are despised. You are still not free. You are hated. From Barack Obama to the neighborhood preacher it is a familiar refrain, straight from the satanic pit of Marxism through the Democratic Party—all in an effort to keep them under control so they can pick votes instead of cotton.

This refrain has made its way into the pop culture of America. According to Black Lives Matter, the NAACP, the Congressional Black Caucus, and Black preachers, Black men are to be pitied, not respected. Police are whooping Black men's behinds all over America. Hollywood, the NFL, and hip hop music all scream in tandem, "White Men Please Stop Whooping Black Men's Behinds." In the movie *Three Billboards Outside Ebbing, Missouri*, the popular refrain in the movie regarding the incompetence of the police is, "It seems the local police department is too busy going around torturing Black folks than to do anything about actual crime." And Black men wonder why they have a hard time acquiring respect. No one touches Vince Everett Ellison.

I've even heard it articulated by these Black leaders that Black people cannot be racist because racism requires "power" and Black people are "powerless." Instead of angrily repudiating this ridiculous mantra, the Black community, amazingly and sadly, have accepted this deadly idea of inferiority and affirmed it through cheers and acclaim. Moreover, the acceptance of the concept of White privilege in the Liberal White community and the mainstream Black community is a backdoor way of codifying White supremacy and Black inferiority under the guise of compassion and care.

Black youth seem to be going backward. The great designer Tom Ford said, "Look at a picture taken in the 1940s and '50s every man had on a suit because they were aspiring." My father, Ivory Ellison and father-in-law, John Calhoun, were such Black men. They graduated from the cotton fields of the South, wearing rags and working outside in the sun. They aspired to be something greater. As young adult men it is almost impossible to find a picture of them without a suit and tie. As they grew older that did not change. They both became very successful in their chosen fields and respected among their contemporaries. They aspired. They hoped. The slave mentality of today was frowned upon. Uplift and pride was being taught. And the Black community achieved.

Now many of the young look homeless. Their outward appearance expresses an inner personality devoid of aspiration, purpose, or hope. A rebellion and an anger has been built after years of hearing from the people they respect the most that they are DESPISED by the world. Like the homeless and destitute, the person that believes this poison does not wear a suit, even when he can afford one. They don't groom or wash themselves. They attempt to disguise defeat as defiance.

Christians, do not be deceived. Jesus's last prayer before his arrest was a prayer of unity among his people. Jesus said in John 17: 20-23:

> My prayer is not for them alone. I pray also for those who will believe in me through their message, that all of them may be one, Father, just as you are in me and I am in you. May they also

believe that you sent me. I have given them the glory that you gave me, that they may be one as we are one.

The Black preachers in these Black churches already know this. They know exactly what they are doing and they do not care. They are the cause behind so much poverty, despair, and death. So long as members of the Black community believe in their own inferiority, they will never accept the mantle of citizenship and freedom. Thus, the Iron Triangle will always speak for and always sell them out.

In Dante's *Inferno,* the ninth and lowest level of hell is reserved for the traitors of Lords. It is called "Judecca" because Judas Iscariot, the betrayer of Jesus Christ, is there. These traitors are conscious, with their bodies twisted in very painful contortions and frozen in ice for eternity. According to Dante, the traitors of GOD are considered the worst people to walk the face of this earth. They are only one step above Satan himself. Therefore, the worst punishment in hell is reserved for them.

Preachers that lead their congregation into the wretched ideology of Marxism, with its hatred of GOD, victimization, and murderous past, and away from the love, forgiveness, and reconciliation of Jesus Christ have committed the highest form of treason.

THE LIE OF SOCIAL JUSTICE

Many Christian ministers have lectured their congregations to support Liberal orthodoxy in an attempt to bring about a Liberal concept called "social justice" and eradicate "inequality." Social justice is society where justice is achieved in every aspect of society rather than the administration of law. It is generally thought of as a world that affords individuals and groups fair treatment and an impartial share of the benefits of society. Sounds great doesn't it? But there is a contradiction. By the previous definition, Liberals supposedly would like the impartial share of benefits and fair treatment of this "just" society to be "achieved" rather than "administered" by law. If this is true, government intervention, which is desired by Liberals in creating this just society, is counterrevolutionary.

Rather, it can only be attained through free markets, the laissez-faire economics of conservatism, or charity and philanthropy. Nevertheless, Liberals remain convinced that they can attain this utopia through government intervention even though it has failed every time they've tried it. You only have to give them control of all of your worldly possessions. They will then determine who deserves what.

In his masterpiece *The Screwtape Letters*, where he is writing a letter from the point of view of a demon, C.S. Lewis in 1942 discussed the fallacy that Christianity should be used as a means toward social justice. He wrote:

> About the general connection between Christianity and politics, our position is more delicate. Certainly we do not want men to allow their Christianity to flow into their political life, for the establishment of anything like a really just society would be a disaster. On the other hand we do want very much, to make men treat Christianity as a means: preferably, of course, as a means to their own advancement, but failing that a means to anything— even to ***social justice***. The thing to do is to get a man at first to value social justice as a thing which the Enemy (GOD) demands, and work him on to the stage at which he values Christianity because it may produce social justice. For the Enemy ***(GOD) will not be used as a convenience***. Men or nations who think they can revive the Faith in order to make a good society might just as well think they can use the stairs of heaven as a short cut to the nearest chemist shop. Fortunately it is easy to coax humans around this little corner.

To be a Christian is to have a personal relationship with GOD and that relationship will put one at perfect peace with the world. A Christian will need the concept of social justice to survive in this world as much as he needs wings to fly. To seek it means that one must violate the Tenth Commandment of "Thou shalt not covet." Modern Christianity is attempting to take GOD'S promise of redemption, salvation, peace, and everlasting life and exchange it for a maxed-out credit card.

Now let's talk about "street money." Street money or walking-around money is cash payments paid mostly to Black preachers from the Democratic Party. Some preachers were paid for each vote produced. Some are paid for speeches made and endorsements. In the book *Bearing the Cross* it was written that in 1960, the Kennedy campaign paid Black preacher, activist, and Harlem Congressman Adam Clayton Powell a sum of fifty thousand dollars for ten endorsement speeches. Powell had previously asked for three hundred thousand dollars. Millions of dollars are spent every election cycle in this way and the politicians get their money's worth. Similar to the days of Martin Luther, a spirit of greed has infested the Church. A prosperity Gospel of materialism has arrived and with it comes its concept of quick wealth, vanity, greed, covetousness, and corruption. Ministers now routinely drive the most expensive cars, wear the most expensive clothes, and live in the most expensive homes, while their members squalor in poverty. Their ostentatious lifestyle has led to a social catch phrase describing them as "pimps in the pulpits." If the reader has any knowledge of Black culture, the reader will understand why the word "pimp" has been applied to Black preachers. The loud pastel-colored suites, along with expensive jewelry and expensive cars will confuse most people if they had to distinguish one from the other—thus bringing to life the old saying, "What feeds a man's vanity teaches as much about him as anything." Nevertheless, greed is not the problem in itself. It is what greed will lead a greedy man to do. This spirit of greed has led Black ministers to be for profit political operatives where they sell or pimp their congregation's votes to the highest bidder. The minister will conveniently forget to mention the politicians usually vote against Church doctrine and simply ask the Church to vote on the basis of race and party. Rich Northeastern or West Coast Liberals bank roll the politicians; they pay the preachers and the congregation is shuffled to the polls sometimes in the church bus.

This is a dirty little secret that has been operating in plain sight since the late 1960s. As a matter of fact, in 1994 after orchestrating a huge upset victory in the New Jersey governor's race for Christine Todd Whitman, legendary Republican campaign manager Ed Rollins got in plenty of trouble when he admitted on nationwide TV to depressing the Black vote by flipping the script on the Democrats and paying some Black ministers in New Jersey not to take their members to the polls on election day. He later recanted the story but the damage was already done. In 2007 it was reported that the Barack Obama campaign was about to lose the Pennsylvania primary because they were unwilling to match the hundreds of thousands of dollars of street money the Clintons were putting on the streets in Philadelphia. They finally relented and pulled out a victory.

It's very simple: the Black community is being pimped for their tithes, their votes, and their freedom. Worst of all it is being done by those that took a vow to protect them. Too many Black preachers play the role of the pimp and too many politicians the role of the John. And for many in the Black community we know what is happening to them.

GOD'S EMISSARY

Being God's emissary on earth is a very demanding job. There is no middle ground in the ministry. To be a man of GOD one has to be sent by GOD. Therefore, a minister is either sent by GOD to deliver his message to mankind or he is a liar. If he is a liar, he is the worst type of liar. If one lies on GOD, he is not only a false profit and an imposter but according to St. Paul he is sent by Satan and is in danger of losing his soul to everlasting punishment. The Bible records in Matthew 7:15-23 the word of Jesus and he said:

> Watch out for false profits. They come to you in sheep's clothing, but inside they are ferocious wolves. *By their fruits you will recognize them . . .* A good tree cannot bear bad fruit and a bad tree cannot bear good fruit . . . Many will say on that day, "Lord, Lord, did we not prophesy in your name and in your name drive out demons and perform many miracles?" Then I will tell them plainly, "I never knew you. Away from me, you evil doers!"

In Matthew 24: 11 he said: "And *MANY* false prophets shall rise and shall deceive *MANY."* In Matthew 24: 24 he warned: "For there shall arise false Christs, and false prophets, and shall shew great signs and wonders; insomuch that, if it were possible, they shall deceive the very elect the

The fiery St. Peter was much more direct. In 2 Peter 2:1 he wrote:

But there were also false prophets among the people, just as there will be false teachers among you . . . Many will follow their shameful ways and will bring the truth into disrepute. In their greed these teachers will exploit you with stories they made up.

Later in the second chapter he described them as "bold, arrogant, brute beasts, creatures of instinct, born only to be caught and destroyed." He said, "They seduce the unstable; they are experts in greed."

In the eighteenth chapter Peter says: "For they mouth empty boastful words and by appealing to the lustful desires of sinful human nature they entice people who are just escaping from those who live in error."

Even St. Paul got into the act. In the book of Corinthians 11:13-15 he described men that preached a different Jesus from the one he and the rest of the apostles preached. He wrote:

For such men are false apostles, deceitful workmen, masquerading as apostles of Christ. And no wonder, for *Satan* himself masquerades as an angel of light. It is not surprising then, if *his servants* masquerade as servants of righteousness. Their end will be what their actions deserve.

Thanks to Martin Luther, Europe experienced its reformation in the 1500s and had come to the conclusion that their preachers were not infallible. They understood that whole institutions could be wickedly compromised and were constantly on guard for the smallest sense of impropriety. Conversely, African slaves still retained their belief in the infallibility of the African holy man. The slave master, knowing this, used it to his advantage. While in Africa the holy man worked for GOD. In America most worked for the slave master.

Naively, Black people believed that no one would profess to be a minister of the almighty GOD who was not specifically called by him. Who would be so wicked or foolish to call down such punishment? It is a person who is either very insane or very evil.

In Africa the holy men were vetted and were given their positions of prestige in the community only after they had shown themselves worthy. But in America their GOD seemed to be the slave master. If slaves were permitted to hear the gospel, the preachers were his paid agents and they worked for the master. In his historical masterpiece, *My Bondage and My Freedom,* Fredrick Douglas wrote regarding plantation life:

> One class of the population is too high to be reached by the preacher and the other class is too low to be cared for by the preacher. The poor have the gospel preached to them, in this neighborhood, ***only when they are able to pay for it. The slaves, having no money, get no gospel. The politician keeps away, because the people have no votes, and the preacher keeps away, because the people have no money.*** The rich planter can afford to learn politics in the parlor and to dispense with religion altogether.

In regard to religion, power attracts extreme opposites. It attracts those who are called to either help or exploit, the strong or the weak, the spirit filled or the flesh filled.

We must take a minister's word regarding whether or not he was sent by GOD. Or do we? Jesus said, "By their fruits you will know them." Let's examine their fruits.

By Their Fruits You Will know Them

It is impossible to understand the workings of the Senate and the Congress with all the intricacies of American politics without studying the Revolution, the Civil War, Reconstruction, Jim Crow, the civil rights movement, and Roe v. Wade or the Supreme Court. In the same manner one cannot understand the influence of the Black preacher on the lives of Black Americans and how that influence was compromised by the White power structure of the South, thereby compromising the development of Black people, unless we go back to the beginning. We have to understand how the deviation of the Black preacher (not Black spirituality) became perpetual.

The role of the Black preacher and his influence in regard to the slaves' march toward freedom, in many ways, has been glorified by history. The facts provide a different picture. Of the more than one hundred million Black Americans that had been enslaved by 1860, history provides very few examples of a Black plantation minister leading anyone to freedom. Actually, it took the guns and bayonets of two and a half million Union soldiers (approximately two hundred and fifty thousand were Black) while Black preachers, for the most part, helped keep Blacks docile and obedient.

The Black preacher, for the most part, looked out for his own self-interest. These deeds were motivated more by the amenities of the slave master and less by the teaching of Christ.

I realize and understand that this line of thinking is tremendously controversial and flies in the face of everything that we have been taught historically regarding the role of the Black preacher. But can we use some logic for a moment?

Even though modern history has been loath to explore and conduct a proper critique of this time in American history, along with logic, there are historical references that verify my suspicions regarding the role of most Black preachers as conduits on the plantation as opposed to resistance fighters.

In the *Dictionary of African American Slavery* (Greenwood Press p. 250) it is written:

Many planters engaged ministers to preach to their slaves, believing that religious instruction was a way to inculcate obedience in the slaves and also to give them some contentment. A group of planters often hired a minister to preach to the whole neighborhood. Ellen Call Long wrote, "It is important to look after the Negro's morals; to instruct him religiously, which is done by **hiring preachers.**" She added, "In the 1830s and 1840s churchmen launched a movement to create plantation missions to bring Christianity to the large majority of rural slaves who remained outside the institutional church's reach. The plantation movement, centered in Carolina and Georgia low country, eventually spread to all slave states. The success of the plantation mission in Florida, as elsewhere, was due in a large way to the appointment of **Negro preachers**, exhorters, and watchmen. These appointees more meaningfully communicated Christianity to slaves than did White preachers, whose doctrine centered upon docility, obedience, and subservience to the White man's rule. Black slave preachers remained cautious and seemingly **preached doctrines approved by Whites**."

W.E.B. Dubois, in his classic *The Souls of Black Folk,* wrote:

By the middle of the eighteenth century the Black slave had sunk, with hushed murmurs, to his place at the bottom of a new philosophy of life. Nothing suited his condition better than the new doctrines of submission embodied in newly learned Christianity. **Slave masters early realized this, and cheerfully aided religious propaganda within certain bounds.** The long system of repression and degradation of the Negro tended to emphasize the elements in his character which made him a valuable chattel: courtesy became humility, moral strength became degenerated into submission, and the exquisite native appreciation of the beautiful became an infinite capacity for dumb suffering.

Historians have said that slavery victimized both master and slave. History records that it created the most warped civilization ever recorded, even to the point where it was referred to as the "peculiar institution." If this terrible institution not only victimized the slave, the master, the economy, and the culture, how could it not also affect the men that had to twist a religion of love to one where one man could be the master over another? Some would say the terrible institution had made victims of the Black preachers themselves.

This sinister, immoral form of control started a fire whose flames still burn and like a virus has permeated every institution of the Black community. American slavery had morphed the Black church almost identically into the past social dynamic that was occurring in Jerusalem at the birth of Christ.

After capturing Jerusalem, Rome wanted a docile and obedient conquered people. Understanding the influence held by the priests of the tribe of Levi (the Pharisees and Sadducees) the Romans formed an alliance. The priests kept the Jews docile while the Romans secured absolute power for the priests. Jesus entered into this dynamic. After the violent cleansing of the temple, he culminated with a historic, pointed, tactless, and curt confrontation between himself and the priests that is recorded in the twenty-third chapter of Matthew. Jesus branded them as hypocrites, blind, and murderers who were greedy and blamed them for the terrible condition of Jewish people. He also prophesied that their false, hypocritical leadership would lead to the destruction of the Jewish people. The priest contacted their partners in crime (the Romans), had Jesus crucified, and continued the exploitation of their people until the prophesy was fulfilled in 66 AD when the temple was destroyed and the Jewish people were scattered.

However, just as there are some good ministers today the Bible reports that there were still a minority of good priests then; two were Nicodemus and Joseph of Arimathea. Both were supporters of Christ and seekers of truth. Nevertheless, the vast majority were compromised. The condition of the people verified this fact.

Sadly, American slavery had injected a virus into the heart of the Black community and America. It made victims of slaves and masters, Whites and Blacks, and preachers and their congregations. Like a living organism it was perpetually reproducing itself. This virus has now spread and like a faulty foundation that supports a home, if not repaired it will soon falter and will destroy everyone inside. Our Bible tells us, "There is nothing new under the sun." The holy man, in league with the politician, is as much a sign of disease as the foam dripping from the mouth of a rabid dog.

True to form this false doctrine of Liberal theology is now infesting other parts of America. There are those now in White America that have migrated from teaching the false gospel of racism to preaching the false gospel of "social justice" and "prosperity" and forego the gospel of repentance and sacrifice. They preach that GOD wants you to be monetarily rich. They speak of Jesus Christ as though he is a "sugar daddy" as opposed to a righteous father willing to forgive the sins of his children once they acknowledge their sin and repent.

Speaking of the false prophets, Jesus said, "By their fruits you will know them." It was very interesting that Jesus did not say, "By their works you will know them." Work is defined as activity in which one exerts faculties to do or perform something.

Fruit is defined as the effect or consequence of an action or operation. Many of the preachers today would prefer that we judge them by their work—that is what they look like, what they are "doing" or what they look like "while" they're doing something. They want us to judge them by the car they drive, the diamonds on their fingers and in their teeth, the clothes they wear, the powerful people they consort with, and the large churches they build. But what are the fruits of all of this work? How are the members of their flock, the African American people, responding to all of this work?

Health
1. On Aug 24, 2014, Fox News reported murder has replaced AIDS as the number one killer of all Black people between the ages of 15 and 34.
2. Over four hundred thousand Black babies are aborted every year. Between 1882 and 1968, 3,446 Blacks were lynched by the Ku

Klux Klan. Today with the help of Black preachers, Black people kill more of their people in three days than the Klan lynched in eighty-six years.

Crime

1. Over 50 percent of Blacks at any time are either in prison, on probation, or on parole.
2. Blacks are seven times more likely than other races to commit murder, and eight times more likely to commit a robbery.
3. Blacks are an estimated thirty-nine times more likely to commit a crime against a White person than vice versa and 136 times more likely to commit a robbery.
4. Between 1980 and 2003 the incarceration rate tripled from 320,000 to 1,390,000.
   Blacks are seven times more likely than Whites to go to prison.
5. Of the top ten most dangerous cities in America all are majority Black.
   (Statistics: New Century Foundation, Oakton VA)

Poverty

1. 2016 poverty statistics report 22 percent of Black families lived in poverty, the highest in the nation, compared to 19.4 for Hispanics, 8.8 percent White, 10.1 for Asian.

Education

1. According to Prep Scholar the average 2017 SAT scores among Black students was 941 compared to 1118 for Whites, 1083 for Asians, 962 for American Indians, and 990 for Hispanics.
2. Colin Powell's nonprofit America's Promise reported that only 52 percent of high school students in urban centers graduate. In cities where the Black populace is extremely high, like Detroit, Cleveland, and Indianapolis, the dropout rate ranges from 65 percent to 75 percent.

Some will say it is not fair for us to blame the Black preacher for the spiritual failings of Black society. If he himself is a victim, how could he be held responsible? He knows whether or not he is called by GOD. I'm sure God would make it unambiguous. Their "fruits" are defined by the condition of their flocks. Do we not blame physicians for the well-being of their patients? Do we not blame businesses for the well-being of their employees? Do we not blame politicians for the well-being of the government? Do we not blame parents for the well-being of their children? Then why shouldn't we blame a preacher for the spiritual well-being of his flock. Maybe the blame should be exponential when they have allowed themselves to be corrupted by elements of society that run counter to everything they profess to believe.

Nevertheless, it is not my role to punish or condemn. That is GOD's business. He did give fair warning to these charlatans. The New Living Translation of the Bible quotes Jesus as saying this in Mark 9:42: "But if anyone causes one of these little ones who trusts in me to fall to sin, it would be better for him to be thrown into the sea with a large millstone tied around his neck."

Do we judge Black preachers for being flawed and as sinful as we are? No. Sinfulness and lack of perfection are never the problem. GOD does not call us to perfection. He calls us to repentance. GOD said he did not punish Sodom for its sin. In Ezekiel 16; 49 GOD is recorded as saying:

Behold, this was the iniquity of thy sister Sodom, **PRIDE . . .** neither did she strengthen the hand of the poor and the needy. And they were **HAUGHTY**, and committed abominations before me: therefore I took them away as I saw good."

Sodom took "pride" in her sin. She made her sin a way of life and flaunted it before God unapologetically. Do any of our Black preachers today reek of this haughtiness and pride with pastel colored pimp suits, ornate jewelry, and ornate lifestyles?

In 1965, it would have been the perfect time for a reformation in the Black church if the tenets of Christianity had still been its goal. The

March on Washington had been a success. The 1964 Civil Rights Act and the 1965 Voting Rights Act had been signed into law. Black Americans in the South were going to vote for the first time since Reconstruction. But that was never the intent of the movement. The movement was designed to subjugate the Black church, not liberate it.

The time had come to move past protest, where the Church had no business, into politics, where the Church still had no business. Politics always has and always will have a corrupting influence on any celestial institution. Since this most sacred institution had been corrupted by slavery and had remained corrupt throughout Reconstruction and Jim Crow the segue was easy.

After 1965 most of the Black clergy sold its congregation to the Liberal wing of the Democratic Party. C.S. Lewis warned us about attempting to use GOD as a means to an end—even if that end is social justice. The civil rights movement was supposedly a Church-led movement. But our ministers, in their quest for social justice, allowed people who hated GOD to use GOD'S Church to press their unholy agenda. Known atheists, Communists, and libertines were allowed to exploit our religion for their own selfish purposes. By selling their congregations the Black preacher sold their souls. They entered into an exclusive contract and picked up where the African slave traders that sold their relatives into slavery some four hundred years before had left off. The Church that had violated its doctrine by guiding Blacks through the civil rights movement was now going to go against its own church doctrine again to support infanticide, sodomy, illegalization of GOD, the destruction of the family, secularism, greed, idolatry, ignorance, and blight. They are deeper in the plantation now more than ever.

The Second Side of the Triangle: The Politician

Again the Devil taketh him up into an
exceeding high mountain, and sheweth
him all the kingdoms of the world, and
the glory of them.

And he said unto him, All these things will
I give thee, if thou wilt fall down and worship me
—Matthew 4:8-9.

In his autobiography *My Bondage, My Freedom*, Fredrick Douglas wrote of an event when he was no more than seven that scarred him for the rest of his life. Under false pretenses, his grandmother walked with him on a twelve-mile journey to another plantation where she, unbeknownst to young Fredrick, was to enslave him to another master and abandon him, never to see him again. After delivering him, his grandmother slipped out of the backdoor of the new master's "big house" without even saying goodbye. His convulsing and crying on the kitchen floor is all young Fredrick could remember. He then began his life as a slave.

Throughout the history of Black America, the most tragic truth regarding Black inferiority is that it was taught to us by our own Black parents, Black churches, and Black society more than White America. When a Black slave girl was raped by her master or overseer it was often the mother that prepared her and delivered her to his door. The child could not be allowed to flout the social norms of their White masters. When a Black child went to a White man's front door, it was usually his mother or father that punished him and told him to go to the White man's backdoor. The child could not be allowed to flout the social norms of the White masters. If a Black child had the temerity to look a White person in the eye, it was usually his parent or grandparent that told the child to look at their feet and not be "uppity." The child could not be allowed to flout the social norms of the White masters. Now, today, if a Black child says he or she will not be a Democrat, it will be the Black parent or Black society that will punish that child for flouting the social norms of the White masters.

Our past tragedies have created a dysfunction where too often there tends to be an unnatural distance between the trustees and their people—the people and their families—the families and their children. The satisfaction of the master is paramount. No Black person can be allowed to flout the social norms of the master. That master has not changed. He is still the White leadership of the Democratic Party. To achieve this absolute obedience the Black community has to conduct itself in the way it always has. The natural affinity to sacrifice, so the child can excel, is very rare. Adults are concerned about their own survival. Too many Black parents sacrificed their children to their masters. The Iron Triangle sacrifices the whole community to theirs. Racist Whites in the Democratic Party have always been the prime beneficiary of this dysfunction salient in our culture. As I have illustrated, this has been a tragic part of Black culture since time and memoriam. Our slavish loyalty to this evil party is destroying Blacks individually and Blacks as a culture collectively. After over two hundred years of this abuse, does this generation have the courage to finally stop it? We will see.

In most leadership relationships, the leaders are chosen and supported by the people they serve. In return, the needs of the people are served. In the Black community this was turned on its head. One example of this is the situation in inner-city public housing. For years the Black and White poor were eligible for housing assistance. Nevertheless, it was a fact that even though White families were almost 80 percent of families receiving housing assistance, you very seldom saw White families in housing projects. Most White families enjoyed the opportunity to get subsidized rent assistance in middle class neighborhoods, while Black Americans were stacked in crowded, diseased, and crime-ridden inner-city housing projects. Most Black people attributed this to White racism but a Black Democrat politician admitted to me that they insisted that these housing projects be placed in their districts and that they be almost exclusively Black. With thousands of poor Blacks trapped in these projects and Black

Democrats controlling everything from food stamps, education, health care, and protection, their reelection was usually assured. The condition of the people was irrelevant. Consequently, this model has worked all over America. Wherever you find a large population of poor Blacks, dependent on government, you will find all of the Iron Triangle in full effect—not because they are trying to help but because they are the cause.

Black leadership found its origins in slavery and continued through a hundred years of Jim Crow. In the book *The 48 Laws of Power* author Robert Greene listed "Do Not Commit to Anyone" as Law number twenty. This law has been consistently broken by the Iron Triangle since 1877. With the KKK eradicated but Democrats still winning almost all of the former Confederate States in the 1876 elections, it seems that Blacks were voting for the party of their masters before Abraham Lincoln was cold in the ground. They've committed to the Democratic Party hook, line, and sinker, and they have rendered the Black community completely powerless. They have developed a dysfunctional system where the party of their former slave masters and current oppressors (the Democrats) choose and finance Black leadership. The Black leaders of today are no different than they were two hundred years ago. Their primary function is to exploit the Black masses for the benefit of their masters. Nothing has changed. Their masters were Democrats then and are Democrats now.

This section will explore:

1. Liberal Democrat political leadership in America and how it came to control and exploit the Black electorate and how they use that control to manipulate enough of the remaining American electorate to control much of the American government.

2. It will explain how a psychological condition called cognitive dissonance or Stockholm syndrome in Black Americans is still responsible for their almost insane loyalty to the Democratic Party.

3. Why other political parties cannot gain any footing in the Black community.

4. Why it is in the best interest of every American, person of faith, and Capitalist to break this stranglehold.

5. Why they are evil and full of hate.

The Democrat Death Cult

When it comes to murder, rape, torture and theft, the Democrat Party is the oldest most prolific and successful organization in history. Slavery was a southern institution and all Slave holders were Democrats. Slavery, Jim Crow and now abortion are enterprises which were all sustained by them. It has been calculated that they are responsible for over 70 million murders, 97 trillion dollars in stolen slave wages, 200 billion hours of forced labor and too many rapes to quantify. Since it's beginning in 1800 the party leadership has been a cabal of psychotics whose main goal has been to provide death on an industrial scale.

Imagine a political party whose 2018 political platform consists of the government funding of child murder, the legality of sexual perversions and pornography, the legalization of illegal drugs, and the promotion of atheism. They have taken the fear and shame of young pregnant mothers and used as fuel for an abortion industry that after 60 million deaths still does not satisfy their thirst for blood. But these mothers are not to blame. They've been led astray and lied to, by people commissioned to help them. This is today's Democratic Party and their iPhone version of the "house negro": The Iron Triangle. For the first thirty years of my life I was a Democrat. Then I discovered these truths. I, like Sheriff Bell in Cormac McCarthy's *No Country for Old Men*, after witnessing an extraordinary amount of violence in his once-peaceful town and contemplating whether to quit law enforcement or become what he had to become to stop it, surmised: "I can't say that it's even what I'm willin' to do. I think it is more like what you are willin' to become. And I think a man would have to put his soul at hazard."

What would I have to become to be a member of today's Democratic Party? I'd have to become a mass murderer of babies! I'd have to become an anti-Christ! I would have to rationalize evil. I'd have to become Esau: a man willing to sell his Birthright for a bowl of pottage. I'd have to become the "Son of Perdition": He as GOD sitteth in the temple of GOD shewing himself that he is GOD. I would have to put my soul at hazard. Some are willing to do it for free health care or food stamps. I won't do it. For any price.

Written in its past and present party platforms are policies supporting slavery, treason, racism, segregation, and murder against the people
of the United States of America. Although the Republican Party has its
problems, you won't find support for any of these monstrosities in their
party platforms. The Democratic Party is responsible for up six hundred
thousand in the Civil War, tens of thousands during segregation, and the
systematic breaking of oaths and Constitutional Law since its inception
in 1792. It has to lie to survive. The Iron Triangle is very helpful in that
respect.

Every year the Democratic Party is responsible for over one million
homicides and unspeakable pain throughout this country. Like slavery
and Jim Crow, they won't stop until we make them. I am hopeful this
work will help reveal the truth to those who can handle it. One must
understand that the Democratic Party was a organization that lived and
breathed Post Modern thought and Subjectivity long before those blasphemous terms entered the Western vocabulary. Like today, in the 1800's,
Democrats believed the law was what they said it was. And even though
the Constitution said that "PERSONS" were protected, Democrats sub-
jectively surmised that Blacks were not people and were not afforded any
protections under the laws of man or GOD (they now say that about
the unborn.) Now, just as then, they admit, that they believe the laws of
GOD and the Constitution are subjective and are what "they" say they
are and can be changed without the consent of the people (they did that
with gay marriage). This ideology is a recipe for chaos, poverty and tyr-
anny. The South was all of that. After the Democrats lost power in the
South, it all changed. Nevertheless, wherever they have found pockets of
power mixed with Black people, the carnage continued. It appears the
Democrats Party has a specific hatred for Black people: They kill as many
as they can everywhere they go.

The Democratic Party reminds me of a splinter group of the Nation
of Islam that call themselves the Five-Percenters. Many members of
their group were inmates during my time as a correctional officer and
I had many opportunities to reason with them. The founder of the

Five-Percenters was a renegade Muslim from the Nation of Islam who went by the name Clarence 13X. The Five-Percenters believe that the Black Man is GOD. Clarence 13X thus changed his name to "Allah the Father" and proclaimed that since the Black Man was GOD, the Black Man could do whatever he pleased, except eat pork. Many of his followers today can be recognized by that same peculiarity: They have "Allah" somewhere in their name and they don't eat pork. Their ideology is the fore runner and template of the modern day Democratic Party with one caveat, most Democrats will eat pork.

The Five-Percenters believed the Black Man could kill whoever he wanted, fornicate with whomever he wanted, gamble and do drugs, etc. Life was subject to their idea of morality, not an objective truth from a higher being. They were that higher being. Ergo, they are GOD. Does this sound familiar? It sounds like the Democratic Party Platform. But even Clarence 13X aka "Allah the Father" didn't believe that he could control the weather. But Democrats believe they can, with climate change legislation.

Nevertheless, Clarence 13X aka "Allah the Father" had a reason for his delusions. He was certifiably insane. Yes! Insane! Let me explain. He was arrested in May 1965 for assault and drug possession. While incarcerated, in July 1965 he was sent to Bellevue Hospital in New York city for a psychiatric examination. In November 1965 he was ruled a "paranoid schizophrenic with delusions of grandeur." That same year he was placed in the Matteawan State Hospital for the Criminally Insane. After the Supreme Court put limits on the confinement of mentally ill patients, he was released in March of 1967. He was murdered on June13th 1969.

The Democrat Party of today is crazier than Clarence 13X, aka "Allah the Father", ever was. Nevertheless, they controlled the House of Representatives; from 2007 to 2011 they controlled Presidency of the United States and from 2008 to 2016 they controlled the entire government of the United States of America from 2009 to 2011. They believe murder is a "choice". "They say, "we are what we say we are, not what science or GOD says we are." Therefore, Democrats are not male or female. They have no color or ethnicity. They say: "We can gamble." "We can do drugs." We can fornicate". "We can walk around naked" "We can confiscate your money, guns, property and children. All without consequence and force everyone to participate against their will, Oh, and they can control the weather. They say: "All women should be believed all men are liars; no presumption of innocence." "The Constitution is a living breathing document. It is, what we say it is". Could it be that the Democrat Party is the political arm of the Five-Percent Nation? Anything is possible.

Was Clarence 13X , aka "Allah the Father" insane? I do not know. But I do know that Clarence 13X , aka "Allah the Father," was locked up in an insane asylum and murdered for believing exactly what the Democratic Party believes today. In other words Clarence 13X , the Five-Percenters and the Democrat Party believe they are GOD!!!! Although it must be understood, the Democratic Party has done a trillion times, more damage to the Black community than the Five-Percenter. If you vote Democrat, you are guilty of supporting this insane foolishness and will be held accountable.

If you wonder what America will look like when it is ruled by those that believe such insanity and adhere to subjective as opposed to objective law, aka the Democrat Party, I would refer you to the Southern United States before 1970. In those dark days because of their subjective beliefs, southern democrat governments murdered their citizens at will. It was a time under Democratic Party subjective law, when lynchings were standard and the powerful, not the law, decided justice. It was a time, when Black citizens could be raped and property could be taken ,with the Democratic Party government as the partner. It was a time when Democrats used the whip, the water hose and the gun to force Black compliance. They enslaved and imprisoned the Black citizenry without due process. It was a time of Democrat "Big Government" control. It was cruel, savage and vicious time. It's the plantation system before 1865; the Jim Crow system before 1970 and the ghetto system today. It was the Constitution under "subjective" not "objective" authority. It is the most dangerous form of government imaginable. It was Hitler and Stalin on steroids.

Ironically, most Black Americans seem to want to remain in those times because every community where there is a large group of Black Americans, they choose to put Democrats in charge. These enclaves then become replicas of the old south. Replete with Black murder on an industrial scale, poverty, police brutality, substandard housings and a Democratic Party overseer with their Iron Triangle House Negroes keeping guard. In these northern plantations, Blacks are treated worse than they were down South before 1970. My fellow Americans, this is our "Back to the Future" not just for Black America but all of America if we do not wake up.

Some would ask, "How did politics in Black community fall to such a point?" First we have to understand that Black politics never had an opportunity to "fall." In order for it to fall it would have at one time been at a higher point. Politics in the twentieth century really began for Blacks in the south after the 1956, 1960, and 1965 Voting Rights Act. Understand that every governor in eleven former Confederate States were Democrats and were viciously opposed to the 1964 Civil Rights Act and Voting Rights Acts. Also, of the twenty-two US senators that represented the states of the old confederacy, twenty-one were Democrats and twenty of the twenty-one voted against the 1964 Civil Rights Act and the 1965 Voting Rights Act. Only Texas Senator Ralph Yarborough voted in favor. Ironically, none of these racist Whites, with the exception of Al Gore Sr., lost their reelection bids after Blacks received the right to vote. More surprisingly Black Southerners joined the Democratic Party. Why?

Could it be that these segregationist Democrats handed out favors, largesse, and decided to let the most trusted Black leaders move in the big house with them? Consequently, every Black politician elected from the old South was a member of the Democratic Party and they, in return, helped them steal the victory from the Black community.

Can anyone picture Jews becoming part of the Nazi party at the end of World War II? Some may say, "Oh, that is such stretch." Well, let us examine the history of the Democratic Party from the beginning and their politics toward Black America.

The Fatal Attraction of the Democratic Party

**"When you believe in things you don't understand you suffer:
Superstition in the way."
—Stevie Wonder**

In May 2012 when Barack Obama endorsed gay marriage many people were aghast that the presumed very religious Black community stood behind him. In fact he lost very little Black support for the many anti-family, anti-life, and anti-religious stances he and his administration took. I was not surprised. I have long since reconciled myself with the sad fact that political party will always trump loyalty to Jesus in most of the Black community. I take no pleasure in saying this but it does illuminate the trouble the Black community is in. Even though their Bible says in Psalms 118:8, "It is better to trust in the Lord than to put confidence in Man," this perverted sense of loyalty to man over GOD seamlessly covers most Black Americans regardless of age, class, income, or area, and is the primary reason for their inability to compete in America.

I was once a Liberal Democrat. My family members were hardcore Christians that took the word of their pastors as the word of GOD himself and the pastor told all of us to vote Democrat. It made sense. All Black politicians were Democrats. All Black pastors were Democrats. All of our church members were Democrats. All of our family members were Democrats, and most importantly, my parents were Democrats. Democrats loved Black people. Everybody, from the doctor that birthed you into the world to the undertaker that buried you, were Democrats. Democrats gave Blacks food stamps, housing projects, integrated schools, and jobs. Democrats told us that Republicans were the devil. They told us that the "R" in Republican stood for "racism" and if we voted for them they would re-segregate all of us and put us back in the cotton fields. Ronald Regan was a racist. Jerry Falwell was the devil. Jesse Jackson was the purist thing on Earth. Abortion was a woman's right. Alternative lifestyles were extensions of freedom and everything wrong in the Black community was the White man's fault. I believed all of this until 1996. In 1996 I was thirty-three years old, and everything started to come together. That was the year I discovered that the Democratic Party was a "death machine."

It is "natural law": when any person, place, or thing finds that it can treat you any way it wants, and it will be accepted by you, you will be disrespected. Likewise, if a respected entity believes there is nothing it can do to earn your favor you will be left to your own devices. This describes the predicament of the Black body politic: Democrats know Blacks will never leave, so Blacks are mistreated and Republicans believe they cannot win their favor so Blacks are left to their own devices.

The history of the Democratic Party since its inception in 1800 can correctly be described as the party of slavery, secession, segregation, socialism and now slaughter. It has always traveled on the dark side of American politics and was willing to take on the cause of any special interest group for a price, no matter how vile. Liberals first recognized Stockholm in the Black population. They understood how they could use the psychological need of Blacks to satisfy their oppressor as leverage to convince them to join the Democratic Party and start working against their own self-interest to press forward the Liberal agenda in America.

THE EXAMINATION

Can the liberties of a nation be thought secure when
we have removed their only firm basis, a conviction in the minds of the
people that these liberties are a gift of GOD?
That they are not to be violated but with his wrath? Indeed I tremble for my
country when I reflect that God is just; that his justice cannot sleep forever.
—President Thomas Jefferson

George Orwell stated, "Who controls the past controls the future, who controls the present controls the past." Regarding the African American community's blind faith in the Democratic Party, former South Carolina Congressman Arthur Ravenel was once quoted as saying, "If Blacks were voting and Jesus ran as a Republican and the Devil a Democrat the Devil would win in a landslide". Oddly before 1964 most Southern Whites reacted identically toward the Democratic Party as Blacks. As Stockholm syndrome dictates, the abused identifies with the abuser. This was because the Democratic Party had one hundred and sixty years of unmitigated racism and terror behind it. There is this myth that the Democratic Party forever lost the South after the 1964 Civil Rights Act. In actuality, Goldwater, the Republican candidate, won only five Southern states in 1964. Nixon won only five in 1968. Jimmy Carter won every Southern state except Virginia in 1976 and Bill Clinton won close to half of the states below the Mason Dixon line in 1992 and 1996. It seemed that most Southern voters were more concerned with the issues than with the party? After 1964, White Southerners became more issue savvy. Nevertheless, most Blacks remained almost exclusively Democratic, no matter the issue.

Most will vote for the Democratic candidate whether that candidate is Liberal, Moderate, or Conservative. They will vote for the Democratic candidate whether the candidate is pro-life or pro-choice, gay or straight, Christian or atheist, civil rights leader or avid racist. They have verified the old adage: "Blind faith in anything will get you killed." Before anything else can change in America this must be rectified.

The schizophrenic relationship between African Americans in the Democratic Party is even practiced among Black separatist groups and so-called Black leaders that many have called racist and anti-Semitic. These individuals and groups rail against White and Jewish oppression. They claim to fight for Black self-reliance and Black control of education. They have called the White man "the devil" and have cursed America, the country of their birth. Yet they turn out the vote for a Democratic Party that currently has as its members the vast majority of Jewish members in the US Senate and US House of Representatives and counted former members of the Ku Klux Klan and openly gay members as part of their leadership. It seems that even these so-called stalwarts of Black independence, rectitude, and high-mindedness cannot overcome the cognitive dissonance and fatal attraction of the Democratic Party. The Black leaders have even adopted their methods of control. As early as 1965 in the book *Professional Bureaucracies: Benefit Systems as Influence Systems*, Richard A. Cloward and Francis Fox Piven wrote:

> The growth of bureaucracies of the welfare state has meant the diminished influence of low-come people in public spheres. This has come about in two ways: first, the bureaucracies have intruded upon and altered processes of public decision so that low-income groups have fewer occasions for exercising influence and fewer effective means of doing so; and second, the bureaucracies have come to exert powerful and inhibiting controls on the low-income people who are their clients . . . The low-income clientele whom the bureaucracies are charged to serve, to placate, and to contain are a special source of sensitivity to them. Any disruption or assertiveness on the part of clients, to the extent that it is visible, will put in jeopardy the support of groups and organizations that watch over the public agencies. The bureaucracies therefore manipulate the benefits and services on which their clients come to depend in such a way as to control their behavior. In this way, governmental benefit systems have become a powerful source of control over low-income people used to ensure the conforming client behaviors which the bureaucracies require both for internal stability and in order to maintain electoral support . . . Today's poor not only have little leverage as workers in economic spheres but have few organizational resources for influencing government and they are increasingly cast into a relationship with institutions of the welfare state which entrenches and reinforces their powerlessness.

This was written in 1965. The Democratic Party was in charge of all three branches of government at that time. Cloward and Piven were telling the government that their government services were enslaving their clientele. Nevertheless, the government continued the process, unchanged, exacting the same results to this day. This is not a mistake.

Furthermore, the Iron Triangle helped orchestrate it.

Why must this be rectified? This blind faith in the Democratic Party is a variation on the original sin of America of slavery. The fact that the party that lost the war to enslave Blacks physically has won the war to enslave them mentally has a wicked irony. These mental chains of slavery still manifest themselves every time a Black person blindly pulls the lever for the party of the Ku Klux Klan, Jefferson Davis, Ross Barnett, and Orval Fabus. The job of securing the mental freedom of all Black people has not been done, and by fiat this mental slavery is spreading throughout the rest of the country. The Democratic Party is using the power loaned to it by the Black community to literally enslave the rest of this nation. America's time to right this wrong is growing shorter and shorter. Moreover, the irony that the remnants of slavery is still the anchor of evil in this country through Black support for the Democratic Party and therefore Liberal/Progressive thought is chilling.

Where did this blind faith come from? How did Black Americans become the enemy of the party of Lincoln and wholly committed to the party of Jefferson Davis? How did Blacks turn against the party that sacrificed three hundred thousand lives to free them, to show respect, loyalty, and devotion to the party that sacrificed three hundred thousand lives to keep them enslaved? Why did Blacks leave the party of Union, freedom, and capitalism to side with the party of slavery, secession, segregation socialism and slaughter?

The hypocrisy of the Democratic Party is other worldly. The opening statement of this chapter was made by an icon of the Democratic Party, who by his own statements would appear to be hypocrites to any serious reader. Jefferson's statements lamenting his conviction that slavery was wrong and America would pay for these past wrongs still did not have the conviction to free his own slaves even after his death. This has been the legacy of the Democratic Party.

Jefferson's question is being answered and the answer is: NO! Liberties of a nation cannot be secure when we have removed their only firm basis, a conviction in the minds of the people that these liberties are a gift of GOD.

Since its inception, Democrats have been a party of hidebound latitudinarianism. In regards to race and freedom, every evil associated with American history has been supported by the Democratic Party. Any insidious or immoral group looking for a political home could find one with them. Theirs has been the home of every failed evil movement in American history. Until 1965 they were the party of slavery, secession, and segregation. Now they are the party of Socialism, atheism, abortion, welfare, genocide, urban decay, alternative lifestyles, illegal immigration, and euthanasia.

THE WILLIE LYNCH SYNDROME, DOLL TEST, AND STOCKHOLM

Democratic control of the Black community in the twenty-first century is a continuation of the mind control phenomenon called the "Willie Lynch syndrome." This phenomenon was designed and mastered by slave master extraordinaire Willie Lynch. It is Stockholm syndrome by another name and is explained in excerpts taken from his speech given on the banks of the James River in 1712 called, "The Making of a Slave." Here are some excerpts.

I greet you here on the bank of the James River in the year of our Lord one thousand seven hundred and twelve. First I shall thank you, the gentlemen of the Colony of Virginia, for bringing me here. I am here to help you solve some of your problems with slaves. Your invitation reached me on my modest plantation in the West Indies, where I have experimented with some of the newest and still oldest methods of control of slaves . . . I have a foolproof method of controlling your Black slaves. I guarantee every one of you that if installed correctly it will control the slaves for at least *three hundred years.*

It is necessary that your slaves trust and depend on us. They must love, respect and trust only us. Whereas nature provides them with the natural capacity to take care of their offspring, we break that natural string of independence from them and thereby create a dependency status, so that we may be able to get from them useful production for our business and pleasure.

When it comes to breaking the uncivilized nigger . . . Take the meanest and most restless nigger, strip him of his clothes in front of the remaining male niggers, the females, and the nigger infants, tar and feather him, tie each leg to a different horse faced in opposite directions, set him afire, and beat both horses to pull him apart in front of the remaining niggers. The next step is to take a bull whip and beat the remaining nigger male to point of death, in front of the female and the infant. Don't kill him. Put the fear of GOD in him, for he can be useful for future breeding.

Take the female . . . If she shows any sign of resistance in submitting completely to your will, do not hesitate to use the bull whip on her to exact that last bit of resistance out of her . . . When in complete submission, she will train her offsprings in the early years to submit to labor, when they become of age. By her being left alone, unprotected, with the male image destroyed, the ordeal caused her to move from her psychological dependent state to a frozen independent state. In this frozen state of independence, she will raise her male and female offspring in reversed roles. For fear of the young male's life she will train him to be mentally weak and dependent, but physically strong.

This former passage is cognitive dissonance explained in sixteenth century terminology.

Native Africans brought to America through the middle passage were forced by murder and torture to give up their language, religion, and culture and adapt to the alien language, religion, and culture of their slave masters. Now that alien language, religion, and culture that their ancestors had to be tortured to accept is so much a part of the Black psyche that Black Americans today would have to be tortured or murdered before they'd give it up.

Likewise, through murder and torture White Southern Democrats have so driven Republicanism and freedom from the minds of the descendants of Republican Freedmen that to this day most Black Republicans have to live in fear and anonymity among their own people.

To better understand the peculiar and fatal relationship Blacks have had with the Democratic Party and why many Blacks describe it as their party, we must first explore briefly the history of the Democratic Party.

THE PARTY OF SLAVERY, SECESSION, SEGREGATION, SOCIALISM AND SLAUGHTER

In 1796 Thomas Jefferson and James Madison started today's Democratic Party. It was called the "Democratic Republican Party" until 1824 when it permanently took the name Democratic Party. The Democratic Republican Party was started waving the bloody shirt of "States' Rights" first espoused by the Kentucky and Virginia Resolutions written by Jefferson and Madison respectively. These resolutions, written in response to the Alien and Sedition Acts, which Jefferson and Madison believed violated the freedom of speech provision guaranteed by the Constitution, were later interpreted by Southern Democrats as their justification for nullification and secession.

The Kentucky Virginia Resolutions basically stated that the Constitution was a contract between the federal government and the states. It stated further that if the federal government enacted any law that any state believed violated the contract, the complaining state had a right to nullify that law. If these violations continued, the contract could be dissolved all together. This theory was quite attractive to Southern slave owners. It was believed by the citizens of the South that the federal government was in perpetual violation of the Constitution in regard to fugitive slave law. They dissolved the Union and started the most destructive war in American history to secure these rights.

THE PARTY OF SEGREGATION

After losing the war you would think the Democrats would have learned their lesson? You would be mistaken. There is an old saying: "A man forced against his will is of the same opinion still." The Democrats had not changed. As usual, they used the forces of darkness to cement their control. Now that Blacks were no longer their property, they had no economic interest in keeping them alive. They resorted to a century of mass murder in an effort to regain and keep their power in the South.

Immediately after the Civil War, Southern ex-slave masters decided to re-educate their newly "freed" slaves into the new social order of the Jim Crow South. This was not going to be difficult for them. Since these newly "freed" people foolishly believed that government had freed them, they compounded the folly by believing that government would protect them. Black Americans make that same mistake today.

For two-hundred years White Democrats had controlled their Black slaves through murder, intimidation, and fear. However, the presence of Union soldiers made this more difficult. Instead of beating and murdering Blacks legally in the open light of day, as they had done before the war, they had to don the disguise of the night rider and carry out their evil in the dead of night. Blacks were running for office and voting for candidates that belonged to the party of their hero, emancipator, and benefactor: Republican Abraham Lincoln. White Southern Democrats refused to live under the rule of the Northern Republicans that had defeated them in the war or their former slaves, who they still considered inferior and less than human.

In Mississippi, White Democrats conceived a plan logically called the "Mississippi Plan."

The Mississippi Plan consisted of three parts. Part 1: Convince, through intimidation and fear, 10 to 15 percent of scalawags to vote for the Democrat candidates. 2. Intimidate carpetbaggers into either voting Democrat or leaving the state. 3. Intimidation of the Black population. Planters, landlords, and merchants used economic coercion with limited success. They unleashed the "Red Shirts" on them. The Red Shirts had taken the place of the outlawed Ku Klux Klan as the military wing of the Democratic Party. The Red Shirts used whippings, intimidation at polls, and murders as tools of control. They provoked riots at Republican rallies and routinely shot and murdered Black Republicans.

The Mississippi Plan was so successful North and South Carolina adopted it. Historians believe that in South Carolina 150 murders were committed in majority Black counties in the weeks leading to the election of 1876.

Lerone Bennett Jr. in his book *Before the Mayflower* chronicled some of these events. He wrote:

> One by one local leaders were killed, driven out of the state, or compromised. In Mississippi, to cite only one case, Charles Caldwell, the courageous state senator, was killed in broad daylight and his body was grotesquely turned completely over by the impact of innumerable shots fired at close range. Nobody knows how many Charles Caldwells died in this period. But Conservative estimates run into the thousands. Albion Tourgee, a White Republican who lived through the counterrevolution, said: "Of the slain there was enough to furnish forth a battlefield, and all from three classes, the Negro, the scalawag, and the carpetbagger—all killed with deliberation, overwhelmed by numbers, roused from slumber at murk midnight, in the halls of public assembly, upon the river bank, on the lonely woods road, in simulation of the public execution, tortured beyond conception. The wounded cannot be counted in this silent warfare.

What did this mean in personal terms? Ex-slave John Childers of Alabama was on the witness stand before members of the US Congress:

—How long after the whipping did she die?
—In eight days.
—How old was she?
—She would have been ten years old on the twenty-sixth of next August.
—Where a colored man is known as a Democrat, and votes Democratic Party, is he ever whipped or interfered with?
—Not at all sir.

—So only the Radicals (Republicans) that are whipped and their children killed?

—Yes, sir; these men that contends for their equal rights for person and property with White men.

—They are the men singled out and punished, are they?

—Yes sir.

—How many of your people in this country do you think have been whipped or otherwise outraged because of their political sentiments?

—O' hundreds, I could not number them to you sir.

Bennett continues:

What made all this enormously effective was superior firepower. Many Democratic clubs owned cannons, which were very useful, oftentimes turning the tide in the endless skirmishes and guerrilla wars fought by Black and White voters. Some Democratic clubs went to the length of rolling out cannons on election days and training them on the polls.

During the final phase of the struggle, Black Republicans could not find work, their wives could not buy supplies, and their children could not get medical attention.

In his book "Chronicles of Black Protest" author Bradford Chambers wrote:

Klansmen marched through towns carrying coffins marked with the names of local Republican leaders . . . A Black man who signed a work contract might discover in it a provision nullifying the contract if he should vote Republican. Newspapers in some counties published the names of Republican voters. The ruthless determination of the Whites is illustrated by the campaign plan of the South Carolina Democratic Party before the elections of 1876. Article 12 of the plan stated: Every Democrat must feel honor-bound to control the vote of at least one Negro, by intimidation, purchase, keeping him away, or as each individual may determine how he may best accomplish it.

Article 16 stated: Never threaten a man individually. If he deserves to be threatened, the necessities of the times require that **he should die**. A dead Radical (Republican) is harmless—a threatened Radical or one driven off by threats from the scene of his operations is often troublesome, sometimes dangerous.

Of course, any free person let alone a person that had lived his entire life as a slave would break under the threat of whipping, starvation, and the murder of his children. But to illustrate just how Black perspectives have turned 180 degrees we must revisit *Before the Mayflower*. It reads:

Rejected by Washington, abandoned by their local allies, and deprived of their leadership by mass assassination, Blacks fell back on their own resources, organizing an extremely effective campaign against wavering Black Republicans. By all accounts Black women were in the forefront of this campaign. Contemporary reports say women were in the forefront of this campaign. Contemporary reports say women refused to marry, date, or cohabit with Black men who weakened and deserted the Republican Party. Landladies evicted Black Democrats. Enraged maidens tore the clothes off "Uncle Toms" who wore the distinctive red shirts of the Democrats, and outraged wives showed their apostate husbands to the door. A South Carolina wife was frank. She did not she said intend to sleep with "a **Democratic nigger.**"

Eventually the federal government told Blacks in the South that it was time for them stand on their own two feet. The federal government could not perpetually defend free grown men against other free grown men. If they were to be free it was time to pay the price of freedom. You must be willing to kill, fight, destroy, and if necessary die or be willing to go back to slavery and pick cotton. Most Black men decided to pick cotton.

Thus, in 1877, after twelve years of Reconstruction, President Rutherford B. Hayes removed all federal troops from the former Confederate states and Whites beat Blacks into submission. Now the descendants of these "freedmen" vote at least 90 percent straight Democrat.

To those who believe the expectation that Blacks fight and defeat their former masters in mortal combat is too much to ask, I refer you to the history of Haiti in the 1800s, Israel in the 1900s, and the United States of America in the 1700s. These nations were formed from outcasts. They were vastly out-numbered, poor, fighting against empires, hated, and despised by the world. Nevertheless, they agreed that they would kill, destroy, fight, and die before ever experiencing slavery again.

It is the irony of ironies. And remarkably, most Blacks do not even know this history. The sorry condition of Black America is completely connected to this conundrum. Black Americans today give almost unanimous support to a party that for the past two hundred years and presently is attempting to destroy them. Today the Black community is stuck at the bottom of every socioeconomic statistic in America. Surprisingly, after two hundred and fifty years many are still servants to the Democratic Party.

"If the Democrats nominate a yeller (yellow) dog I'll vote for him," retorted Theodore Hallman at the Louisville Democratic convention in 1900. He made this statement to indicate his undying support for the ideals of the Southern Democratic Party. Most of these ideals rested on the party's absolute dedication to segregation and the debasement of Blacks. This phrase gained national prominence when many White Southerners supported presidential candidate Alfred Smith in 1928 even though there were several items that they were uncomfortable with (including his Catholicism). During the Jim Crow era of the South this phrase became the rallying cry because this party supported, organized, and participated in the murder, torture, and pseudo-slavery of Blacks.

Now, ironically, this rallying cry has become a staple of Southern Blacks. Why? The usual response to such a dynamic would be umbrage and an absolute visceral reaction to the party, its members, its slogans, and symbols. Why did Blacks latch on to the Democratic Party and become its most loyal members? Stockholm syndrome and cognitive dissonance.

It is a natural response to identify with one's oppressor in order to survive. The environment previously described is absolutely palatable to that end. It is understandable why and how Black Americans became brainwashed into the Democratic Party. It must also be acknowledged that this nation decided that the remedy to this problem was to forcibly integrate these Black citizens with the same White Democrats who viewed them as inferiors. This more than anything explains the current condition of Black Americans.

THE PARTY OF SLAUGHTER

"Although volume upon volume is written to prove slavery
a very good thing, we never hear of a man who wishes to take good
of it by being a slave himself."
—Abraham Lincoln

"Whenever I hear anyone arguing over (the good of) slavery, I have a
strong impulse to see it tried on him personally."
—Abraham Lincoln

I'm reminded of these quotes by Lincoln whenever I hear a Democrat defend the crime of abortion. I am reminded that the Democratic Party supported slavery and now abortion with the same demonic logic and the holy logic of Christ exposes it as immoral. So let's use the holy logic of Christ on abortion: how many Democrats would have chosen to be aborted? Probably the same amount that would have chosen to be slaves.

No government should finance the murder of its own citizens. Nevertheless, according to Supreme Justice Anthony Kennedy there have been sixty million abortions in the United States since 1973. The African American population is responsible for approximately thirty-five million. Approximately thirty-five million African American children have been killed. The Democrats want to kill more. They have a proabortion plank in their party platform. They would fund the abortion of every child in the world if they could. They are currently pushing for legislation to extend abortion until childbirth and after childbirth. You would have to be blind to not see the hand of Satan in all of this. Defeat at the polls is the only thing that will stop them. Make sure you check these facts for yourself. Because, as of now, everyone that reads these words and still votes for a proabortion Democrat or Republican (of which there are very few) is complicit in homicide and infanticide. One day you will stand before GOD and have to answer for it.

The good news: If you have knowingly voted for a proabortion candidate in the past: repent. There is room at the Cross. All will be forgiven. Pride will tell you that you have nothing to repent. Do not believe it. Pride always comes before the fall. Confess. Repent. All will be forgiven.

Most women and most Americans are not the cause of this tragedy. They have relied on false information provided by people of authority, knowledge, and gravitas. In law and in our Bibles we are told that someone else can cause you to sin. Jesus said, "If anyone cause one of these to sin it would be better that a millstone be tied to his neck and thrown into the sea." With this in mind, imagine a young woman frightened, alone, and pregnant going to a Democratic doctor, politician, civic organizer, or preacher for advice. Will they say, "That baby is a child of GOD, keep it and we will help you raise it." Or will they say: "That thing in your body is nothing. We will pay you to get rid of it."

The most prominent Democrats in America will tell this young woman to kill her child and tell her there will be no repercussions for it in this life or the next. These Democrats are the cause. They will be the ones that pay the cost.

THE MYTH OF BROWN VS. BOARD OF EDUCATION

By 1905, Black Tuskegee University had produced more self-made millionaires than Harvard, Yale, and Princeton combined. This astounding statistic was reported in the February 23, 2017, edition of *Forbes Magazine*. Nevertheless, Stockholm syndrome-suffering Blacks have always believed that the White man's ice was colder and his fire was hotter.

Economic conditions and educational opportunities have nothing to do with integration. The activists that pushed for integration were all mostly upper middle class and college educated. It was all about two diametrically opposed concepts: power and inferiority. Liberals leveraged the false promise of equality to an "inferior"-minded population to acquire "power" for themselves. Brown vs. Board of Education is another chapter in that sad story.

Did you know that Black inferiority is written into the law of the American judicial system? A Black civic organization, the NAACP, sued the Clarendon County School system in South Carolina (and others) for the right to forcibly send Black children to public schools with White children and be taught by White teachers. You read correctly: South Carolina. The state that started the Civil War. The result was Brown vs. Board of Education, the landmark case where the Supreme Court ended racial segregation in public schools and confirmed this nation's belief in Black inferiority and Black Americans belief in their own inferiority.

About Brown vs. Board of Education, Dr. Martin Luther King Jr. at least got this right when he was quoted in the *NY Times* as saying:

I favor integration of public accommodation and travel. I am for equality. However, I think integration in our public schools is different. In that setting you are dealing with one of the most important assets of an individual: the mind. White people view Black people as inferior. A large percentage of them have a very low opinion of our race. People with such a low view of the Black race cannot be given free rein and put in charge of intellectual care and development of our boys and girls.

The myth of Brown vs. Board of Education persists in the misconception that the Supreme Court ruled in favor of the plaintiffs because of the inadequate building, curricula, qualifications, and salaries of teachers in the segregated Black school systems all over America and that Brown integrated the schools in an effort to ensure that Blacks and Whites received equal protection and excess. The logic was that if Blacks and

Whites attended the same schools, everything at the schools would be equal and their educations would be equal. Nothing could be further from the truth. Brown was not about equal excess to education. Brown vs. Board of Education was in fact an attempt to cure Black America's inferiority complex by facilitating the federal takeover of local education to enforce integration compliance

To expel the myth that the Brown case was decided to increase Black student achievement, equalize buildings, curricula, qualifications, and salaries of teachers, one need only to read Chief Justice Earl Warrens Opinion. In it he stated:

In the instant cases, that question is directly presented. Here, unlike Sweat v. Painter, there are findings below that the ***Negro and White schools involved have been equalized, or are being equalized, with respect to buildings, curricula, qualifications, and salaries of teachers and other tangible factors in the Negro and White schools involved in each of the cases.*** We must look instead to the effect of segregation itself on public education.

According to the Supreme Court, the problems that have existed in Black public schools since 1970 did not exist before Brown. There was no achievement gap, there wasn't any crime, the teachers were not inferior, and the facilities were equal. As a matter of fact, in my home town the segregated Black high school, Carver High, was a newer and more modern school than the White school, Haywood High School. But Carver High had to be abandoned because of Brown.

Chief Justice Warren then went on to explain the real reason for Brown vs. Board of Education when he wrote:

We come then to the question presented: Does segregation of children in public schools solely on the basis of race, even though the physical facilities and other "tangible" factors may be equal, deprive the children of the minority group equal opportunities? We believe it does . . . To separate them from others of similar age and qualifications solely because of their race *generates a feeling of inferiority* as to their status in the community that may affect their hearts and minds in a way unlikely ever to be undone . . . *Segregation of White and Colored children in public schools has a detrimental effect upon the colored children.*

I was not born in 1956 but my parents were students in the Black schools of that era and the Supreme Court decreed that my parents were inferior. The Iron Triangle and White Liberal benefactors were jubilant. Ironically, the Supreme Court case overturned by Brown, the infamous Plessy vs. Ferguson, surprisingly did not extoll Black inferiority as I had been taught all of my life. After discovering that I had been lied to about so much in our history I decided to double check even subjects that I had previously left unchallenged. I found that Plessy actually affirmed Black equality. Justice Brown opined in Plessy:

We consider the underlying fallacy of the plaintiff's argument to consist in the assumption that the enforced separation of the two races stamps the colored race with a badge of inferiority. If this be so it is not by reason of anything found in the act , but solely because the colored race chooses to put that construction upon it. The argument necessarily assumes that if, as has been more than once the case, and is not unlikely to be again, the colored race should become the dominant power in the state legislature, and should enact a law in precisely similar terms, it would thereby relegate the White race to an inferior position. We imagine that the White race, at least, would not acquiesce in this assumption. The argument also assumes that social prejudices may be overcome by legislation, and that equal rights cannot be secured to the Negro except by an enforced commingling of the two races. We cannot accept this proposition. If the two races are to meet on terms of social equality, it must be the result of a natural affinity, a mutual appreciation of each other's merits and a voluntary consent of individuals . . . Legislation is powerless to eradicate racial instincts to abolish distinctions based upon physical differences and the attempt to do so can only result in accentuating the difficulties of the present situation. If the civil and political rights of both races be equal, one cannot be inferior to the other civilly or politically. If one race be inferior to the other socially, the Constitution of the United States cannot put them upon the same plane.

No matter its reputation or intent, time has proven this statement to be correct. The Plessy "decision" was despicable. The law should be color-blind. Nevertheless, its above "opinion" is logically sound and a truthful analysis will conclude it has been proven correct by history.

In the social environment of 1896 Blacks should have been seeking the protection of Plessy. Most White people during that time were uncivilized toward Blacks. Black Americans needed separation from them. Whites didn't need protections from Blacks. But Black Stockholm syndrome and cognitive dissonance would not allow that. Nevertheless, Blacks celebrate Brown because even though it calls them inferior, it allowed them to forcibly integrate with their former masters. And even though Plessy screamed Blacks were equal, Blacks rejected it because it didn't force Whites to be with them. Plessy said this integration would have to occur naturally not by law or government decree. It also forewarned that government interference would only exacerbate the situation.

I must make one thing perfectly clear: segregation of children in public education solely on the basis of race is not only wrong it is immoral. I support the Brown "decision" not the Brown "opinion." Brown's decision to dismantle racial segregation implemented by law was right. But their opinion that the raising of Black self-esteem was the rationale behind their decision was racist, presumptuous, condescending, and legally wrong- headed. The fact that many Black Americans accepted this decision may prove that the Supreme Court may have been right about the inferiority complex of many Blacks but to assume that forced personal contact with White children would cure it had no basis and in fact and has been born out by today's evidence. Moreover, there were many Black Americans who considered the Brown opinion completely insane. Many

Blacks still do not understand why some Blacks wanted George Wallace and the KKK to educate their children. It was like Jews turning their children over to the Nazis.

This opinion about Brown is widely shared in the Black community but the Iron Triangle won't allow it to be discussed in the mass media. Black author Ibram X Kendi wrote in his best-selling book, *Stamped From the Beginning*:

> Warren essentially offer a racist opinion in this landmark case: separate Black educational facilities were inherently unequal and inferior because Black students were not exposed to White students . . . Despite its basis in racist reasoning, for many—and of many did not actually read Warren's opinion—the effect of the landmark decision overturning Plessy vs. Ferguson honored Black people."

In addition to this, the education of Black children has gotten much worse since Brown. Black teachers were giving Black children such great education that educational achievement was not even argued in Brown vs. Board of Education by the NAACP. Even though Black schools were underfunded and teachers underpaid, Black children were getting a better education than White children in the South. James Meredith told me, "The Black education in America before integration was the best educational system in the world." Now there is an achievement gap. And the Doll Test, the test that provided the most empirical evidence of the devastating effects segregation was having on Black children, still summons the same results today whenever taken by Black children. The Doll Test itself proves the existence of Stockholm syndrome in mass polluting the Black community. And in a sort of irony it gave Liberal Whites insight into the Black psyche in a way that they had never had before. At first they "thought" most Blacks would do anything to just be in their presence. Now they "knew it" and wielded this weapon like serine gas: odorless, colorless, and tasteless.

Ironically, on Sept. 14, 2017, the *Seattle Times* published a story highlighting a study by the UCLA Civil Rights Project with the head-line "Segregation worse in schools sixty years after Brown vs. Board of Education." In addition, the *Washington Post* reinforced the belief that Black inferiority is still a serious part of Liberal orthodoxy. Regarding Black underachievement sixty years after Brown, they cited a study by Richard Rothstein, a research associate at the Economic Policy Institute. He reported:

> Schools remain segregated today because neighborhoods in which they are located are segregated. Raising achievement of low-income Black children requires residential integration, from which school integration can follow. Education policy is housing policy. Federal requirements that communities must pursue residential integration have been unenforced, and federal programs to subsidize movement of low-income families to middle-class communities have been weak and ineffective. Correcting these policy shortcomings is essential.

No one can be this stupid! They want to continue the policies of the past sixty years. They are not trying stop it! They want more of it! The status quo is what they want!

So, what was it all for? Brown vs. Board of Education was a backdoor way for the federal government and the Liberals to take control of public education. After the Supreme Court ruled that public schools had to integrate with "all deliberate speed" the decree needed an enforcement authority. That authority was the US Government and the Liberals that work for it. Before Brown, the education of children was a local affair. The feds had very little to do with it. After Brown the feds took control. After Brown they changed the mission of public education from education to indoctrination. Consequently, in the years after Brown, our country has consistently spiraled downward compared to other nations in the industrialized world. Paul E. Peterson, a professor of government at Harvard University, put it this way:

> Americans who went to school during the 1960s ranked a respectable third; those schooled in the 1970s ranked fifth. But sixteen to twenty-five-year-old adults who were wandering America's school hallways during the 1980s and 90s ranked fourteenth. In short, the literacy survey records a simple steady progression downward.

By 2017, the *Hechinger Report* reported the USA was last in education among industrial nations. With Liberal and federal control the schools threw out religion, prayer, discipline, and teacher quality. The schools became money-making enterprises for unions, politicians, bureaucrats, and a training camp for the Liberal indoctrination of all children.

Today the Iron Triangle still celebrates Brown vs. Board of Education the way Christians celebrate Christmas. Thurgood Marshall was catapulted to the Supreme Court and the NAACP become world-renowned. Movies have been made about it. Books have been written about it. Plays have been acted on Broadway. And it is all a lie! Black education was not inferior. Black facilities were not inferior. Black teacher pay was not inferior. Black people just felt inferior and most of them still do. The education of Black children is worse because of Brown. The education of all children is worse because of Brown. America is worse because of Brown.

Our children are being sacrificed on the altar of Liberalism courtesy of the Iron Triangle and the Democratic Party.

BLACK AMERICA'S GREATEST ENEMY

In the South, from 1800 up until 1965, the Democratic Party had been the greatest enemy to Black people in world history.

In 1860 when the South succeeded from the Union every Southern senator that voted for succession was a Democrat and every Southern congressman was either a Democrat or an Independent Democrat. In 1860 the Democratic Party had existed approximately sixty years with a primary goal, as far as Blacks were concerned, of sustaining, protecting, and expanding slavery and the hatred of Blacks. All of these Democrats were willing to go to war to protect the most vicious and barbaric institution the world had ever known.

The genesis of the Republican Party, on the other hand, was contrived to destroy the institution of slavery. In response to the passage of the Kansas Nebraska Act and the Dred Scott Decision, Abraham Lincoln, William Seward, Horace Greely, and other Northern Democrats and anti-slavery Whigs started the Republican Party in 1856.

Since that time there has never been a word written in the party platform that can be perceived as negative against Black Americans

After the Civil War, Black freedmen became Republicans while most Whites retained their Democratic pedigree. In order to control Blacks and intimidate them from voting Democrats employed the services of the KKK and the Red Shirts. Historian Dr. Eric Foner said, "In effect the Ku Klux Klan was a military force serving the interest of the Democratic Party and all who desired the restoration of White supremacy." As a matter of fact, according to J.C. Lester and D.L. Wilson two of the interrogation questions of a prospective Klan member were: Are you opposed to Negro equality both social and political? Are you or have you ever been a member of the Radical Republican Party or "The Grand Army of the Republic?" If you answered yes you could not become a Klan member.

The facts are, Southern Democrats repressed the Black Republican vote through intimidation and murder and destroyed all opposition parties in the South for one hundred years. The Democrats, with the Ku Klux Klan as their military wing, ruled the South until 1965. But with television, Black anger, world attention, global Communist competition, and strong Northern support, the tactics of the KKK could no longer be tolerated. But how could Democrats, who could no longer use intimidation as a tactic to openly suppress the Black vote, stay in power?

DEMOCRATS FIGHT AGAINST MARTIN LUTHER KING AND THE CIVIL RIGHTS MOVEMENT

The saddest irony of this most perplexing loyalty that Blacks have for the Democratic Party exists in the covert program of espionage and sabotage during the civil rights movement against its leaders called COINTELPRO. COINTELPRO is an acronym for Counter Intelligence Program that was authorized by the Justice Department of Democrat John F. Kennedy, supervised by Democrat Attorney General Bobby Kennedy, and administered by unaffiliated J. Edgar Hoover. COINTELPRO spent millions of dollars and man hours surveilling and audiotaping the hotel rooms of Dr. Martin Luther King Jr. They had a directive from the Kennedy administration to disrupt the civil rights movement, discredit its leadership, and prohibit the emergence of a "Black Messiah." Wikipedia reports regarding COINTELPRO:

> In the case of Black activists the FBI and police threatened, instigated, and themselves conducted break-ins, vandalism, assaults, and beatings. These attacks including political assassination were so extensive, vicious, and calculated that they can accurately be termed a form of official "terrorism."

This did not happen in a vacuum. The FBI had ample evidence that the civil rights movement was led by and in the control of the Communist Party. The idea of SCLC was formed by two of the top Communists in America: Stanley Levinson and Bayard Rustin. A few of the other secret Communists connected to King and the civil rights movement were: James Dombrowski, Aubrey Williams, Abner Berry, Carl Braden, Anne McCarty Braden, Pete Seeger, and Hunter Pitts O'Dell. President John F. Kennedy warned Dr. King that he was under surveillance and that if his connection with these Communists became public knowledge it would destroy the movement and his presidency. Kennedy considered it suspicious that King would partner with a group whose stated goal was to wipe all religion from the face of the earth and the end of Democracy. He demanded that he cut ties with these Communists. King said he would but did not—thus, the surveillance. To this day the civil rights movement actively maintains these ties. Now Communists and most of their values are the platform of the Democratic Party.

President Kennedy's attempts to save his party from this takeover was in vain. His most famous statement: "Ask not what your country can do for you, ask what you can do for your country," is anathema to today's Democratic Party. Most Democrats only want to complain about and leech off of their country. The FBI, heeding the history lesson of Communist revolutions in Russia, China, and Cuba, were not going to take any chances with Dr. King, the members of the civil rights movement, and their Communist partners. The gloves came off.

During testimony of the House Subcommittee on Assassinations it was discovered that in early January 1966 the FBI had sent some of these secret tapes to the SCLC office, where they were discovered by Dr. King's wife. Along with these tapes existed a letter that, in addition to accusing Dr. King of being a "fraud, an imbecile, and evil immoral beast," it also said "King, you are done . . . There is only one thing left for you to do. You know what it is." This letter was written by the FBI while it was under the auspices of the Democrat Lyndon Johnson Administration. Some of you may believe that the Kennedys and Lyndon Johnson did not know about the goings-on in the FBI. Even when *American Gangster* on Black Entertainment Television (BET) highlighted J. Edgar Hoover as a gangster because of his connection to COINTELPRO, the subject matter of the show suggested that Presidents Kennedy & Johnson along with their attorneys general knew nothing and once they found out could do nothing about it. The evidence suggests otherwise: the Select Committee to Study Governmental Operations With Respect to Intelligence Activities and the Rights of Americans states:

> Officials in the Justice Department and White House were aware, however, that the FBI was conducting an intelligence investigation, not a criminal investigation of Dr. King and that the FBI had written authorization from the attorney general (Bobby

Kennedy) to wiretap Dr. King and SCLC offices. The FBI had tapes embarrassing to Dr. King that they offered to play for the White House . . . In the light of what those officials did know about the FBI's conduct toward Dr. King, they were remiss in failing to take appropriate steps in curbing the bureau's behavior . . . those officials must share responsibility for what occurred . . . Yet President Johnson did not order the investigation terminated.

There have been constant conspiracy theories, especially in the Black community, that Dr. King was assassinated by the US government. But in these theories exist a twisted logic that can only manifest when accompanied with a psychosis: If Dr. King was killed by the government in 1968 (and there is no definitive evidence that he was) then he had to be killed by the Democrats, because they were the party in charge of the executive branch of government from 1960-1968. Nevertheless, the psychosis in Black America is so powerful I feel comfortable in saying that even if the conspiracy was discovered to be fact many Blacks would still not be able to break their blind obedience to the Democratic Party.

For sure, I am not suggesting that Blacks should exchange their blind faith in the Democratic Party for blind faith in the Republican Party. Neither party is worthy of any American's blind obedience. But I am suggesting it is important that all Americans start to think and vote their values and not out of tradition or loyalty. Black Americans are relaying to men a status that should only be reserved for GOD.

THE DEMOCRAT GOLEM OF 1965

In his 1965 report to President Johnson, Daniel P. Moynihan wrote "the bipartisanship of the Black leadership was one of their major strengths." But after Dr. King's death most of his colleagues sold the entire Black electorate to the Southern wing of the Democratic Party. Since then, the Democrats as a party have continued to gravitate to the dark side of American politics in an effort to survive. They have become the scavengers and enablers of our government. They have made a Faustian deal with the golems of the Liberal world. What other party has in its ranks those who have the support of: abortionists, pornographers, libertines, drug-legalization advocates, atheists, Socialists, child molesters (NAMBLA), radical feminism, eugenicists, Ku Klux Klan members, COINTELPRO, and state control of our children.

Blacks have been delivered back into the hands of a people who have shown themselves to be our mortal enemy. The previous statistical evidence provides ample proof that we have been losing ground ever since.

THE BAIT AND SWITCH

Envy thou not the oppressor,
and choose none of his ways.
—Proverbs 3:31

An old South Carolina Democrat White supremacist politician who will remain nameless once told me, "If we (the Democrats) would have known that the Blacks would vote for the Democrats in the way that they have, we would have allowed them to vote a long time ago. As bad as we treated them, we knew they were going to vote for those damn Republicans. But they won't and for the life of me I don't know why."

Democrats have not changed. They have changed us. In the same way they supported and fought to maintain the immoral policies of the past three centuries they are still in the business of mingling their hands in the blood of the innocent. Their Liberal wing is the force behind the over one million abortions performed in this nation yearly. They are the force behind the gay marriage and transgender movement. They are the force behind the pornography and sex industry (Ask Larry Flint of Hustler and Hugh Hefner of Playboy which party they support.) At Hugh Hefner's death Rev. Jesse Jackson praised the help he gave himself and Martin Luther King during the civil rights movement. That's right, Dr. King hung out with pornographers. They are the force that are trying to force GOD out of the public square. They are the force behind a criminally dysfunctional public educational system that causes ignorance, poverty, family breakdown, victimization, and violence. Our Black politicians support the same disgusting politics under the auspices of elected representation.

Let me make one distinction here: Liberals are more the problem than Democrats. Most Liberals just happen to be Democrats. Liberalism, whether it is Republican or Democrat, is the bane of our existence. But why did Liberalism take root in the Democratic Party but not the Republican Party? Someone once said, "If a man is a crook, you need only to pay his price." The same goes for a political party.

The ideology of the Republican Party has not changed since its inception in 1856. They believe in smaller government, law and order, individual responsibility, and strict adherence to the Constitution.

Through Liberalism, the Democrats had employed the perfect ideology to seduce the Blacks of 1965. Black leaders buoyed by the success of the March on Washington, the 1964 Civil Rights Act, and the 1965 Voting Rights Act—events that seemed more than impossible only ten years earlier—could easily be seduced into believing that they could force the US Government into providing them with food, housing, medical care, and a guaranteed income for life. After all, didn't they deserve it? After four hundred years of slavery, rape, and murder, why should they have to wait any longer?

Furthermore, the millions of dollars that the Kennedys, Rockefellers, teamsters, and other Liberals had invested in the civil rights movement came with strings attached and would pay off in dividends when Black civil rights and the left combined to press forward a Socialist agenda. A hodgepodge of groups that previously had nothing in common used the civil rights movement as a cause célèbre' and capitalized on the opportunity to ingratiate themselves to millions of uneducated voters.

Blacks believed they had achieved their freedom through the civil rights movement. They believed they had achieved equal opportunity. Now they wanted to achieve "equality." By equality, Black leaders did not mean equal opportunities or equal protection under the law. No, they meant equal results. Bayard Rustin, a former Communist and a leader in the civil rights movement, stated, "It is now concerned not merely with removing barriers to opportunity but with achieving the fact of equality." This was new and almost Marxist in its thinking. But it also coincides with the far-left Liberal thinking of that time and filled an inward desire of the bourgeois Black civil rights leaders to be like their former masters. Whether this is right or wrong is irrelevant but to say it is not true would be disingenuous at best. In his book *Bearing the Cross*, in the chapter "Economic Justice and Vietnam 1966-1967," David J. Garrow wrote of the movement:

> Now the movement would have to pursue "substantive" rather than "surface" changes, and would be "making demands that will cost the nation something" because they would raise "class issues"—"issues that relate to the privileged as over against the underprivileged." At the heart of the matter, King stressed, was the fact that "something is wrong with the economic system of our nation . . . ***something is wrong with capitalism.***" It was a belief he had long held but rarely stated in public because of the obvious political dangers. "I am not going to allow anybody to put me in the bind of making me say, every time I said there must be a better ***distribution of wealth***, and maybe ***America must move toward a Democratic socialism.***"

The problem is that equality is essentially a red herring in a meritocracy. It is an ideology that is primarily coveted by the losers in society and propagated by con men. It ensures the practice of Blacks determining their standards of success by comparing themselves to another race will always indicate by default that they consider themselves inferior to that race. For Blacks to say in one voice that they are proud of being Black and they are as good as anyone but then say in another voice that they consider themselves unequal to Whites because they do not match them in some arbitrary standard is worse than schizophrenia.

In the book *The Triple Package*, authors Amy Chua (Tiger Mom) and Jed Rubenfeld tackled this dilemma:

At least since Brown v. Board of Education and the civil rights acts of the 1960s, America's official racial mantra has been equality. You can criticize America's ideal of this as unfulfilled—some might even call it hypocritical—but its premises are clear and noble. All individuals are equal; every race is equal; every group is just as good as every other . . . But the dirty little secret is that the groups enjoying disproportionate success in America do not tell themselves, "We're as good as other people." They tell themselves they're better . . . In a paradoxical sense, equality isn't fair to African Americans. Superiority is the one narrative that America has relentlessly denied to or ground out of its Black population, not only in the old era of slavery and Jim Crow, but equally in the new era of equality . . . It's one thing for a group with a longstanding superiority complex to pledge allegiance to the idea of universal equality. After all, a group's silent belief in its own superiority isn't fundamentally altered by this declaration; indeed, as they proclaim the equality of all mankind, members of such a group can pride themselves on their generosity and open-mindedness (showing just how superior they really are). It's quite another thing for a group with a long history of inferiority narratives behind it to be asked to pledge the same ideal.

THE DANIEL TEST

Before June 21, 2018, The World Health Organization (WHO) considered gender incongruence and gender identity disorder as pathological. What changed? Pressure from affluent Liberal/atheist lobbying groups and Liberal/atheists in western governments saw an opportunity to push conflict between western nations and their religious citizens and forced the policy change—even though the vast majority of Black Americans disagree with these lifestyles. The Iron Triangle takes its orders from Liberal masters and has given full support to their goals. Many doctors still agree this is a mental disorder.

As these people struggle, Christians must not do as Liberals, parading and displaying them to take advantage of their pain—encouraging them to mutilate themselves. Let's hold them up in LOVE, prayer, and compassion, knowing that the TRUTH, not lies, will set them free. Evil will always try to convince you to be comfortable in your shortcomings. Good will force you to master your shortcomings, force you out of your comfort zone, and help you aspire toward your true purpose.

Liberals care as much about these people as they do for Black people. On September 14, 2018, when the American Academy of Pediatrics reported 51 percent percent of transgender male adolescents and 30 percent of transgender female adolescents attempted suicide they did not expand treatment for the mental disorder; they expanded government programs to exploit their mental disorder. They increased government funding to encourage these human beings to slice off and add on unlimited body parts, then called it compassion. Liberal Democrats and the Iron Triangle will exploit their pain in the same way they exploit Black pain: to raise money, get votes, sow discord among people of faith, add numbers to the ranks of the government-dependent, and expedite the downfall of America. In addition, it is the latest attempt by Liberals to apply the "*Daniel Test*" to America.

The "*Daniel Test*" derives its name from an incident recorded in the Bible in the Book of Daniel, chapter 6. While exiled in Persia, Daniel was raised to high office by his royal master, Darius the Mede. His jealous rivals set a trap for him. They knew Daniel only prayed to his GOD. They knew he very astute, very disciplined, and very loyal. They would use this against him.

Daniels rivals convinced Darius to issue a royal decree that for thirty days no prayers should be addressed to any god or man but Darius himself. Anyone that broke this law would be thrown to the lions. They had Daniel in their trap. If he obeyed the King, he would be abandoned by his GOD. If he obeyed his GOD, the king would kill him. Either way, Daniel would eliminated. Daniel, of course, did not comply. Darius reluctantly had him thrown in the lion's den, where he survived all night. His rivals then took his place in the lion's den and were eaten.

Liberals and the Iron Triangle covet the passing of legislation contradicting Christian, Islamic, and Jewish doctrine for this same reason. When they press for limitless abortion, LGBTQ rights, and restrictions on religious liberties and then use the power of government to enforce these policies, people of faith are left with a conundrum: either imprisonment, denial of some government service, or disobedience to their GOD.

Their primary goal is to make honesty illegal, turn facts into lies, and slowly use the power of government to turn its citizens against GOD. Time, science, and communication will prove that the LGBTQ movement is the legalization and government promotion of a mental disorder, the origin of which rests in the concept of self-hate. Time, science, and communication will prove that abortion is the murder of children and true Christians will be recognized by their willingness to support or condemn this one issue. Time, science, and communication will expose the Iron Triangle here on Earth. Their exposure will lead them to lash out against all that is good. But they will not prevail. But for them there is also good news. They can repent and return to GOD. All will be forgiven.

BLACK CIVIC ORGANIZATIONS

(THE THIRD SIDE OF THE TRIANGLE)

Legend tells us that African American civic organizations land somewhere between Jesus and Elvis on their scale of importance in American life. Like the Bible, it is considered blasphemy to criticize or question their intentions and outcomes. These organizations are responsible for some of America's greatest hits: Brown vs. Board of Education, the Montgomery Bus Boycott, Selma, and the March on Washington 1963. However, most of these organizations are led by people who are either insane, immoral, or incredibly stupid. They haven't changed their tactics or goals in sixty years.

The goal in this chapter is not to chronical the origins of every civil rights and civic organization over the past one hundred years. Anyone can find that information with a Google search. They have been portraying themselves falsely and I will expose their true intent, which can only be realized when their fruits are examined.

Nobel Prize-winning economist Gunner Myrdal examined the genesis of Negro leadership in America in his masterpiece *An American Dilemma*. He described it this way:

> The White caste has an obvious interest in trying to have accommodating Negro leaders to help them control the Negro group. Under no circumstance, in any community where the Negro forms a substantial portion of the total population, are the attitudes and behavior of the Negro a matter of no concern to Whites . . . Some are quite frank in wanting to keep Negros from reading the Constitution or studying social subjects. Whites have seen their possibilities of controlling the Negro masses directly greatly diminished. The Whites have increasingly to resort to leaders in the Negro group. They have, therefore, an interest in helping those leaders obtain as much prestige and influence in the Negro community as possible—as long as they cooperate with the Whites faithfully."

Ergo: White Liberals started Black civic organizations to service the needs of White Liberals. This arrangement still exists.

This chapter will highlight that the real goals of African American Civic Organizations are to serve the wishes of their Liberal White benefactors. The National Association For the Advancement of Colored People (NAACP), the Southern Christian Leadership Conference (SCLC), Black Lives Matter, National Urban League, the National Action Network, and Rainbow Coalition are just a few.

It will highlight that they are:

1. Funded by left-wing White Liberals that exploit Blacks for their purposes.
2. Advocates for political positions that are harmful to the Black community but advantageous for Liberalism.
3. Heavily invested in keeping Black America uneducated, poor, victimized, and dependent.

4. Populated by Blacks who are only puppets and figure heads.
5. In league with the Democratic Party.
6. Evil and full of hate.

Consider this: Blacks supposedly hate Republicans, yet these groups encourage Black people to vote for candidates who will put Republicans in charge of their health care, education, and safety. Even though Black people are the subject of more violent crime, racism, and police brutality than any group in America, these groups encourage Black people to disarm and relinquish their Second Amendment rights and depend on the police that are supposedly brutalizing them to protect them. Even though Black people have the lowest-performing, most violent and crime-ridden schools in America, these groups encourage Blacks to vote for politicians who will trap their children in these schools, denying them school choice and a chance at a better life. Even though Black people are the most unemployed and underserved portion of the American community, they are encouraged to vote for politicians who support the unrestricted flow of illegal immigrants into their community. The result is more competition for scarce jobs and puts further strain on government services that are already breaking down. Even though the scourge of drugs is destroying much of the Black community, they encourage Black people to vote for people intent on legalizing marijuana and providing free needles to shoot up heroin. Even though the family and religion has been the only sustaining elements of the Black community, they encourage Black people to vote for politicians who have a record of trying to destroy it all. Even though Black people believe that GOD made everything and it was good, they encourage Black people to vote for politicians who believe gender is a choice and government dollars should be used to change men to women and women to men and back again in perpetuity. Even though we see our children grow in the wombs of their mothers, we feel them move and we see their faces, these people tell Black people to support candidates who claim not only that their children are not alive but they are seeking government funding to kill every last one of them. Even though it has been proven that the Theory of Evolution is racist, un-Christian, and statistically impossible, Blacks continue to vote for people who will propagate this lie to their children in public schools while at the same time denying them the opportunity to pray or even study the Bible as a historical document. The support of this lie is eroding our respect for life, science, and GOD.

In the book *1984* George Orwell wrote that the government will so completely train its citizens that without thought they will accept any official statement as true. They will even believe 2+2=5 and disregard the past fact that 2+2=4. In the book *1984* Orwell wrote:

> In the end the Party would announce that two and two made five, and you would have to believe it. It was inevitable that they should make that claim sooner or later: the logic of their position demanded it. Not merely the validity of experience, but the very existence of external reality, was tacitly denied by their philosophy. The heresy of heresies was common sense. And what was terrifying was not that they would kill you for thinking otherwise, but that they might be right. For, after all, how do we know that two and two make four? Or that the force of gravity works? Or that the past is unchangeable? If both the past and the external world exist only in the mind and if the mind itself is controllable what then?"

I thought it was impossible until I witnessed the eight Obama years and what Liberal Democrats did to the Black community and how the Iron Triangle help facilitate heresy.

I saw a cult of personality in Barack Obama (a Liberal Democratic politician) emerge and be sustained by the Iron Triangle. I saw his picture beside Jesus Christ in Black churches. His face tattooed on their bodies. They were buried in clothing with his name and picture on it. His picture hung in their homes. It was like I had awakened in the Stalinist Soviet Union or Saddam Hussein's Iraq, where the picture of the dictator is forced to be on display everywhere. Like Staubach said of Ahab in *Moby Dick*, "I saw a madman beget more madmen!" They told Black America that up was down and down was up and they gladly accepted. I saw, in disbelief, as men that I respected and women I adored got caught up in this Liberal hysteria, where they gave a Democratic hack politician reverence that should be reserved only for GOD. The Liberal Democrats had made an African American man president. Black Democrats made him the "Son of Perdition," the man that set in the seat of GOD and made himself GOD. Obama determined when life began. Obama determined gender. Obama determined who lived and died. Obama decided what bathroom you could use. America survived eight years in Akrasia (land of insanity).

Why would they do it? It serves the needs of their White Liberal benefactors. They are a tool and facilitator for their evil. They can then watch the country burn. And it did burn. From Baltimore, to Ferguson, to Occupy Wall Street. It burned.

This causes me to believe the Liberals are achieving every one of their goals. There were two divergent views regarding the direction for Blacks after 1965. One led to freedom; the other to dependency. One would lead to responsibility; the other to victimization. One led to the logical reflex of self-preservation and the other to the cowering degradation of Stockholm syndrome. The road to freedom and responsibility came in a March 1965 report by the Office of Policy and Research of the United States Department of Labor and submitted by future US Senator and Harvard Professor Daniel Patrick Moynihan and by future presidential candidate and consumer activist Ralph Nader. The other came from the left leaning Liberals who were in control of the civil rights movement and therefore Black America. This is when Black America lost its way.

The Moynihan report, considered quite controversial at its time, was written for the Lyndon Johnson administration. It was entitled "The Negro Family: The Case For National Action." The report chronicles the journey of Blacks in America from 1765 through 1965 and explains in great detail the enormous toll the barbaric system of slavery played in damaging Black society. The report begins by admitting:

In this new period the expectations of the Negro Americans will go beyond civil rights. Being Americans, they will now expect that in the near future equal opportunities for them as a group will produce roughly equal results, as compared with other groups. This is not going to happen. Nor will it happen for generations to come unless a new and special effort is made. There are two reasons. First, the racist virus in the American blood stream still afflicts us . . . Second, three centuries of sometimes unimaginable mistreatment have taken their toll on the Negro people.

Sellout 1965

These things happened. They were glorious and they changed the world
And then we f**ked up the end game.
—Congressman Charlie Wilson

Congressman Charlie Wilson made this statement referring to how the United States helped Afghanistan defeat the Soviet Union in the 1980s and how the United States allowed Afghanistan to fall to terrorism and eventually become the launch pad for 9/11.

Black Americans did the same. We awoke the manhood of Black America and could have used the power of the federal government to build a nation within a nation but the Iron Triangle screwed up the end game by asking for forced integration and government control. Now things are worse. This sellout is highlighted in the following pages.

The End Game

The Moynihan Report chronicles the journey of Blacks in America from 1765 through 1965 and explains in great detail the enormous toll the barbaric system of slavery played in damaging Black society and how the federal government could assist in fixing it. Nevertheless, the prominent civic organizations of that era, which are still very active today, obeyed the orders of their White Northern Liberal masters and rejected this report and it's recommendations that **"the Black father"**

must be head of his household and that "the Black family" had to be preserved. These two outcomes were never the goals of these civic organizations or the Liberals that controlled and funded them. Matter of fact, they were directly opposed to them. Control of the Black vote was their primary goal. Evidence of this is present in a letter sent to Dr. Martin Luther King by one of the founders of the Southern Christian Leadership Conference (SCLC), and according to the FBI, the number one Communist in America, Stanley Levinson.

Stanley Levinson was a White New York lawyer who filed the paperwork that started the SCLC. He also negotiated Dr. King's book deals and raised money for the SCLC. He also helped edit and write his books. It is rumored that he wrote most of the "I have a Dream Speech." While editing Dr. King's book, *Where Do We Go From Here*, Mr. Levinson let Dr. King know that the SCLC should not be concerned with Negro improvement. They should be only concerned with the vote. In the book *Bearing the Cross* David Garrow recorded it this way:

> **"_On voting and registration you mention nothing, which is a serous omission_.**" Other subjects that King had emphasized should be left out, Levinson advised. In particular, "the section on **_Negro self-improvement is undesirable_** . . . The goal should be to activate, and organize people toward the main objective rather than appeal for change of character separated from the pursuit of social goals."

Understand, this comes from the White, Northern, Liberal, man who started and funded the SCLC. They pretended that they were involved to improve the plight of Blacks. No! Many were revolutionaries who wanted to control the Democratic Party. The Black vote was their ticket.

There was only one way this could happen They knew this control of the Black community rested in the destruction and castration of the father. Consequently, the leaders of theses civic organizations rejected the Moynihan Report's recommendations and instead started a fifty-year war on the Black man and the Black family that culminated in problems we never experienced before in such volume.

The thesis concluded that the problem was not just economic and political, as the many Black preachers and Liberals leading the civil rights movement had concluded. Moynihan concluded that the problem consisted in the fact that slavery had destroyed the Black family as an institution and all the ills of Black society germinated from this corrupt seed and were perpetual. Moynihan continued:

> A national effort is required that will give a unity of purpose to the many activities of the federal government in this area, directed to a new kind of national goal: the establishment of a stable Negro family structure. This would be a new departure for federal policy. And a difficult one. But it almost certainly offers the only possibility of resolving in our time what is, after all, the nation's oldest, and most intransigent, and now its most dangerous social problem. What Gunnar Myrdal said in *An American Dilemma* remains true today: "America is free to choose whether the Negro shall remain her liability or become her opportunity."

He also presented evidence that AFDC program (welfare) in the way that it was set up was starting a dependency in government programs that was troubling. Moynihan wrote:

> On the other hand our study has produced some clear indications that the situation may indeed have begun to feed on itself. It may be noted, for example, that for most of the post-war period male Negro unemployment and the number of new AFDC cases rose and fell together as if connected by a chain from 1948 to 1962. The correlation between the two series of data was as astonishing. (This would mean that 83 percent of the rise and fall in AFDC cases can be statistically ascribed to the rise and fall in the unemployment rate.) In 1960, however, for the first time, unemployment declined, but the number of new AFDC cases rose. In 1963 this happened a second time. In 1964 a third time.

After reporting a tremendous amount of statistical information to support his claims regarding an unsettling pattern that was going to lead to more destruction of the Black family and therefore thwart any gains in the civil rights laws, Moynihan wrote:

That the Negro American has survived at all is extraordinary— a lesser people might simply have died out, as indeed others have . . . What then is the problem? We feel the answer is clear enough. Three centuries of injustice have brought a deep-seated structural distortion in the life of the Negro American. **At this point, the present pathology is capable of reproducing itself without any help from the White community.** The cycle can be broken only if these distortions are set right . . . In a word, a national effort toward the problem of Negro Americans must be directed toward the question of family structure. The object should be to strengthen the Negro family as to enable it to raise and support its members as do other families . . . Since the widespread family disorganization among Negroes has resulted from the failure of the father to play the role in family life required by American society, thus perpetuating itself without assistance from the White world. Mitigation of this problem must await those changes in the Negro and American society which will enable the Negro father to play the role required of him . . . But here is where the true injury has occurred; unless this damage is repaired, all the effort to end discrimination and poverty and injustice will come to little.

Moynihan had nailed it. Liberalism, in the way of unlimited social programs, would not repair the damage done to the Black community or make them self-sufficient in this competitive environment. Evidence that these Liberal civic organizations have never had any intention of providing a road map to Black independence is provided in the formula that is relied upon for success in their own belief system. Liberals believe strongly in the science of psychology, because many psychiatrists are atheist and believe more in the power of man than the power of GOD. I don't put much faith in their science. Nevertheless, I know that psychiatry is religion to the Liberal. Bearing that in mind, one would believe that psychiatry should be used as a road map to help to the average Liberal. They know these theories like the back of their hand and give homage to them as we do to GOD almighty. When it comes to their lives, they follow these edicts as though they were the Ten Commandments. But when it comes to Blacks, the people they were to lead out of the wilderness, these edits become suspiciously absent. For example:

Maslow's hierarchy of needs theory states that human motives are arranged in a hierarchy, with the most basic needs at the bottom. At the top of the list are the most developed needs (esteem needs) and finally self-actualization at the end. In order to achieve self-actualization, the stage where a human can achieve their full potential, the four lesser stages must first be fulfilled. These stages include:

1. Physiological needs: These include food, water, sleep, and sex.
2. Safety needs: Security, protection, and the avoidance of pain.
3. Belongingness and love needs: These needs focus on the affiliation with other people, affection, and feeling loved
4. Esteem needs: We also need to respect ourselves and to win the esteem of other people. Otherwise we feel discouraged and inferior, according to Maslow; we will not strive for the highest level of hierarchy.
5. Self-actualization needs: A person who has satisfied all the lower needs can seek self-actualization, attempting to reach her or his full potential.

Even though Liberals know these five steps to fulfilling one's potential, if they really had the best interest of Blacks or Americans at heart one would have to ask why their plan leaves most of Black America stuck at number three on the scale. The scale clearly explains that a person needs to accomplish number four, esteem needs, before they can reach number five, which is self-actualization. Esteem needs says: We also need to

THE IRON TRIANGLE

respect ourselves and to win the esteem of other people. Otherwise we feel discouraged and inferior, according to Maslow; we will not strive for the highest level of hierarchy.

With the Liberal Black civic organizations' promotion of forced integration, government handouts through welfare, and quota systems through affirmative action programs, how can Black people achieve respect for themselves and win the esteem of others? The absence of this fourth need guaranteed Black inferiority and guaranteed the continuation of Stockholm.

It is impossible to reach the fourth step if Blacks follow the plans established by these Liberal civic organizations. The evidence provided by Dr. Maslow, one of their Liberal icons, concludes that Liberal civic organizations know that they are not leading Blacks to a position where they can achieve self-actualization, nor will they lead the children they are educating toward that goal. They leave them somewhere between number one and number two, where they are always attempting to satisfy their need for food, water, sleep, sex, protection, security, and the avoidance of pain. They know that self-actualization can only be achieved when Blacks become independent and self-sufficient. Liberals therefore must thwart this at all costs, for they know that once Blacks receive this enlightenment it will be almost impossible for them to be controlled by them. Their experiment in Black America has worked splendidly. Their results are excellent. They have 90 percent of Black Americans under their control. They don't have me. They are now targeting the rest of America.

"MAN OUT OF THE HOUSE"

For this reason, when Liberals read the Moynihan report they exploded! They slammed the report and in the *Journal of Public History*, 2002, William Grabner accused Moynihan of "propagating racist views." They also accused him of "blaming the victim," a phrase coined by psychologist Dr. William Ryan and the author of a book bearing the same title. They would use this phrase if anyone suggested that Blacks had any part in their plight. Because of course, to admit that Blacks had any part in keeping themselves down would also mean that they had the power to pull themselves up. And Liberals always need a victim.

In March 2014, former Speaker of the House and former vice-presidential nominee Paul Ryan remarked on Bill Bennett's radio show there was a "tailspin of culture in our inner cities in particular of men not working and just generations of men not even thinking about working or learning to value the culture of work." Immediately, as if on cue, the Liberal establishment accused him of "blaming the victim." The Liberals never change.

The most powerful voices in the Black community slammed the Moynihan report and his idea to use federal funds and power to build the Black family. President Johnson instructed Moynihan to brief the civil rights community on the report and incorporate their endorsement. He took the opportunity to do so at the first Ford Foundation-funded Ministers Leadership Programs. According to David Garrow in the Book *Bearing the Cross* Dr. King had largely endorsed the study and its preferred outcomes and suggested it be presented to the rest of the civil rights community. But the other Black ministers, Black civic leaders, and their Liberal masters had other ideas. On page 598 of *Bearing the Cross* David J. Garrow writes about a heated session between Daniel P. Moynihan and the civil rights leadership regarding his report:

> Moynihan spoke in an "atmosphere of total hostility," one Ford Foundation observer reported, and Moynihan later wrote to Ford President McGeorge Bundy to protest SCLC's venture (the Poor Peoples' March). The session was "the first time I have ever found myself in an atmosphere so suffused with near madness . . . The militants who consistently stated one untruth after another (about me, about the United States, about the president. About history, etc., etc.,) without a single voice being raised in objection. King, Abernathy, and Young sat there throughout, utterly unwilling (at least with me present) to say a word in support of nonviolence, integration, or peaceableness." Ford's observer noted that it was an accomplishment that Moynihan "got out alive."

In this rejection lay most of the ills of the Black community and most of the collateral damage throughout America. According to Alma Carten, in the August 22, 2016, *New Republic Magazine* they called it "**The Man In House Rule.**" It required welfare workers to make unannounced visits to determine if fathers were living in the home—if evidence of a male presence was found, cases were closed and **welfare checks discontinued**. It provided a disincentive to marry and for fathers to have any contact with their children. It didn't just declare war against fatherhood, it declared war against Black men specifically.

To intentionally take a boy's father away destroys him as a child, futuristically as a man, and negatively effects his descendants in perpetuity. To provide perverse incentives to a mother to not marry and a family to separate is worse than atomic war. The Japanese recovered from the atomic bomb in less than twenty years. It has been fifty years since this attack and the wound is still fresh. The Iron Triangle of the civil rights movement (the Black preacher, civic organizer, and politician) and the Liberal Democratic Party were the architects of this masterpiece. This was not a mistake. In the past, to keep their slaves on the Democratic Plantation they had resorted to war, rape, and murder. "Man In House" was easy. It was evil brilliance. They planned it all. They were the assassin and made America and White Christian Conservatives the patsy and have fought like hell to expand it every year since.

My historical critique of how the plantation slave culture had perpetually distorted the function of Black leadership and how they see themselves as conduits between a strong White community and a weak Black community explains the reaction of most civil rights leaders to the Moynihan report. But most importantly, it illustrated one of the most extreme and pivotal aspects of Liberal ideology put into action: the destruction of marriage and the traditional family in America. Liberals in the civil rights establishment took advantage of this historical period, when the remaking of Black America was being negotiated in the federal government, by initiating their primary goal of destroying the traditional family in America by destroying the Black family first. For this to happen, the weakening of the father figure was imperative.

This may sound extreme but one must understand, White feminists, who gained more from the civil rights movement than any other minority group, see marriage as oppressive toward women and fought for no-fault divorce, a man-out welfare system, and infanticide. In his paper "Beyond Gay Marriage" author Stanley Kurtz describes how Liberals have always seen marriage and family as a barrier to their aims and as something that needs to be destroyed

Conversely, while in 1965 Moynihan touted stabilization and the saving of the Black family as the primary goal of the federal government, before 1990, civil rights groups, Black preachers, and Liberals very seldom listed it as a problem and very few, if any, even addressed it.

As of 2008, the websites of the perennial civil rights organizations NAACP, SCLC, Rainbow/Push, Urban League, and CORE mention voter registration, economic empowerment, integrated public schools, adequate distribution of government benefits to African Americans, etc. But they never mention the uplift of the Black family. They would say that if their plans were implemented it would by default benefit the Black family. The last forty years have proven that to be one of the greatest miscalculations in world history.

These were not good people. According to a 2017 FBI document dump, it was revealed that a Black Minister who attended a workshop in Miami to train ministers in February 1968 expressed his "disgust with the behind-the-scene drinking, fornication, and homosexuality that went on at the conference." In the same document dump it was revealed that Communists had written in their newspaper, "Communists will do their utmost to strengthen and unite the Negro Movement and ring it to the backing of White working people." The FBI said King and his organization were "made to order to achieve these objectives." For those that believe this accusation untrue, I refer you to the undeniable fact that the Black community in America is still operated like a Communist State and the moral fabric is worse than ever.

Black leadership was and is so completely compromised that in 2006 when Bill Cosby challenged the Black community to take responsibility for their community and chastised fathers for their lack of leadership, the

Liberal elite went into convulsions. His statements made national news. And immediately the Black leadership castigated Cosby for "blaming the victim." Consequently, the protections he enjoyed from his Liberal friends evaporated and as of this writing he is in prison.

The Liberals who hijacked the civil rights movement had every intention of taking advantage of the voting bloc of millions of undereducated and naive Blacks who had never voted before and had been socialized to blindly follow their leadership. The promise of a Christmas-like payout of government welfare would be the reward for their blind allegiance. Remember, as I wrote earlier, Ronald Kessler in his book *Inside the White House* wrote about a meeting, witnessed by Air Force One steward Robert MacMillan, between Lyndon Johnson and Southern governors, where President Johnson was asked about his support for civil rights. He wrote:

> Johnson, like other presidents, would often reveal his true motivation in asides that the press never picked up. During one trip, Johnson was discussing his proposed civil rights bill with two governors. Explaining why it was so important to him, he said it was simple: "I'll have them niggers voting Democratic for two hundred years." "That was the reason he was pushing the bill," said MacMillan, who was present during the conversation. Not because he wanted equality for everyone. It was strictly a political ploy for the Democratic Party. He was a phony from the word go.

Even Bill Moyers a Johnson Administration assistant, told a Select Committee to Study Governmental Operations with Respect to Intelligence Activities:

> "That the Johnson Administration's willingness to permit the FBI to continue investigation of Dr. King also appears to have involved political considerations". Moyers continued that President Johnson: "was very concerned that his embracing the civil rights movement and Martin Luther King would not backfire politically."

The Democrats had conducted their homework and knew that on the aggregate the country was ready for the passage of civil rights legislation. In 1968 the Democrats were not hurt by civil rights. They were hurt by Vietnam and the emergence of a Liberal West Coast/Northeastern counter-culture that infiltrated their party through civil rights movements and changed it from a party of racism and hate to a party where there are no taboos and everything is permitted.

Moynihan's report was filled with logic and historical and statistical data. Nevertheless, the federal government decided to push Black Americans in a completely opposite direction. Liberal civic leaders in the civil rights movement were convinced the goals of the SCLC's "Poor Peoples March on Washington," scheduled for May of 1968, was the way to go. And Moynihan's plan completely contradicted it.

According to David Garrow, Dr. King admitted to his ideology:

"Speaking to the Breadbasket staff, King 'asked us to turn off the tape recorder,' " one participant recalled. "He talked about what he called Democratic socialism, and he said 'I can't say this publicly, and if you say I said it I'm not gonna admit to it,' And he talked about the fact that he didn't believe that capitalism as it was constructed could meet the needs of poor people, and that we might need to look at was a kind of socialism but a Democratic socialism."

Dr. Martin Luther King Jr. was one of the greatest figures in US history. Would a twenty-first century Dr. Martin Luther King Jr., after seeing the devastating effects of Liberalism in the Black community, have continued down that road? Would he have accepted the moral and religious breakdown of the Black community as it stands today? Hindsight is 20/20 and in 1968 these concepts had not been vetted as they have now.

Also, being in the constant company of Communists, Marxists, and Socialists without a doubt had an effect on his social theory during the sixties. But the evidence shows that Dr. King had the ability to reevaluate his position and change his strategy as he did after Albany, Georgia, and on the Vietnam War when his goals were not met. To the Liberal everything is color, gender, or sexual preference. For Black people to believe otherwise is folly.

But at this time in history, the moral authority of Black leadership and a remedy for Black oppression was being leveraged by Liberals to push the Democratic Party, the Black community, and America toward Socialism. It does "appear" these Black leaders were Socialist. I "know" they weren't economists. So maybe they did not understand the economic repercussions of their actions. But these were men of the South. They had been victims of Southern authorities all of their life. In 1965 the GOVERNMENT meant "White men." In 1965 most government was local. Therefore, in the South, GOVERNMENT meant Southern, racist, White men, and Black leaders still coveted the control of White men .

The SCLC plan demanded that the GOVERNMENT: Provide three hundred billion dollars of annual appropriation for comprehensive anti-poverty efforts but an absolute minimum would be congressional passage of (1) a full employment commitment, (2) a guaranteed annual income measure, and (3) funds for at least five hundred thousand units of low-income housing per year.

After four hundred years of oppression from "the government" that systematically violated the US Constitution, what led these men to believe this same government would now magically provide for them with no strings attached? The old saying "Beware of Greeks baring gifts" was well forgotten. Our Black leaders were in a game over their heads. They were playing checkers and the Liberals were playing chess. The Liberals had a completed the psychological profile of their victims and knew their victims much better than their victims knew themselves.

The words of Priest Dr. Don Felix should have been remembered when he said of Liberals and Liberalism:

It is not only through the avenues of disordered passions that this spiritual disease may gain entrance; it may make its inroad through the intellect, and this under a disguise often calculated to deceive the unwary and incautious. **The Trojans admitted the**

enemy into their walls under the impression that they were actually securing a valuable acquisition to their safety, and today their fatal experience has come down to the proverb— "Beware of Greeks when they bring gifts." Intellectual torpidity, ignorance, or even virtues such as benevolence, generosity, and pity may be the unsuspected way open to this foe and lo we are surprised to find him in possession of the Citadel!

Their sin is not that they made a mistake in 1965; it is that they have not reevaluated their position as others have. They have in fact continued their assistance in the fratricidal onslaught that is destroying Black America and has bled into the nation.

I do not know whether it was their Stockholm syndrome, their greed, their pride, their ignorance, or a mixture of all of them that caused our Black leaders to return their people to their enemies after such a hard-fought victory. I know they played the Black community well. Through the vote, Blacks delivered to Liberals the keys to this nation and the Black community received poverty, prison, and death in return.

THE UNMASKING

I took my children to Washington, DC, in an effort to have them experience the real history of this country. While walking through this majestic city and reading the inscriptions written on the monuments my children gathered an intimate knowledge about each monument and the message it was attempting to portray the people who erected the monument and the message they wanted future Americans to salvage from their time in history. We read the words spoken by Lincoln and how he credited GOD for his guidance in the Civil War. We read the words of Jefferson and how he credited God (NOT GOVERNMENT) for granting us our rights. Then I visited the Martin Luther King Jr. monument. Immediately, I noticed that the word reverend was not used in his name nor the fact that he was the leader of the Southern CHRISTIAN Leadership Conference anywhere on the monument. As I continued to read the quotes of Martin Luther King Jr. I finally realized that the word GOD or Jesus was not mentioned anywhere on the monument. It had to be very difficult to find anything of substance said by Dr. King that didn't mention GOD, Jesus, or Lord. As a matter of fact, the last speech he ever gave he said, "I want to do GOD'S will" and "Mine eyes have seen the glory of the coming of the LORD." Amazingly there hasn't been any outcry from the Black politicians, the Black civic organizations, or the Black preachers (The Iron Triangle). This was not overlooked. They are admitting that the civil rights movement was not GOD-led as pretended?

There was an outcry when the *Washington Post*'s Rachel Manteuffel reported that the quote on the monument was a paraphrase not an exact quote. The quote on the monument had read: "I was a drum major for justice, peace, and righteousness." Dr. King's actual quote was: "If you want to say I was a drum major, say that I was a drum major for justice. Say that I was a drum major for peace. I was a drum major for righteousness. And all of the other shallow things will not matter." Mrs. Manteuffel argued that the revised quote misrepresented who King was. The *Post*'s editorial board and poet Maya Angelou also agreed. They believed the "if" clause that is left out is salient and changed the meaning completely. On January 13, 2012, the US Secretary of the Interior Ken Salazar ordered the quotation be corrected. It cost between seven hundred thousand dollars and nine hundred thousand dollars to accomplish.

Sometimes important things are revealed in silence. The fact that they went to all of this trouble because of the word "if" well illustrates that GOD was left out intentionally. Believe me, if the mostly White *Washington Post* Editorial Board could pressure the US Government to change the King Monument, the SCLC, NAACP, Black Caucus, and President Obama could have had a statue of Jesus erected beside him if they wanted. But they have been as quiet as church mice about all of this. Conclusion: GOD is not important to them. This proved they are exactly who I say they are. This was their monument. It belonged to the White Liberal establishment. On orders from their White Liberal Democrat masters, Obama ordered that the monument be changed to what they wanted and they did not want GOD anywhere to be seen.

They see America as they see King's monument: White and Godless.

Their Liberal White masters are in the process of telling the truth about their part in our history. Many of them saw King as a chitlin-eating pawn and a hayseed. But there is no doubt King saw himself as a preacher, and would be offended that a monument honoring him did not mention that he was a reverend, the leader of the Southern Christian Leadership Conference and his Church, or any mention of GOD in the thousands of statements attributed to him.

In his book "*Parting the Waters*" author Taylor Branch wrote Martin Luther King was a "Pawn of History". In fifty years people will know the truth. This was not a Christian Church-led movement. This was a Christian Church-exploitation movement. They must keep Black people in the Democratic Party and attaching something to their GOD is the greatest endorsement they can achieve. They must whitewash Muhammad Ali, Malcolm X, and Hughey Newton. We don't have to go over all this again. Go to Dr. King's monument and understand how he is being marketed to push the Liberal agenda in America.

It is not the goal of this book to relitigate the personal failings of our civil rights icons. I have attempted to deal with them mostly on policy, but it cannot be ignored that since morality and justice were part of the civil rights movement and it leaders were anything but that, it's results should not be surprising. It was essentially a garbage in, garbage out movement. We have worshipped GOD's with feet of clay. Now there is a reckoning, and the payment is more than we can bear.

If the reader is so inclined to read more on this subject, there are three books that delve into the personal character of those that led the movement. They are: *Parting the Waters* by Taylor Branch, *And the Wall Came Tumbling Down* by Ralph Abernathy, and *Bearing the Cross* by David Garrow. These books will give you more insight regarding the personal conduct of those that volunteered to lecture America on the failings of her conduct while they were process of betraying their people.

The good news is they are being exposed. This book is the beginning of a new awakening. A younger generation is coming of age. They will not be as easily swayed by the infallibility of false prophets or the false belief that integration cures everything. They are smarter and less trusting than their parents. They have the advantage of hindsight and history. They will tear down the foundations of these White Liberal organizations that parade in blackface. They will still exist but we will view them as we viewed country sharecroppers, the KKK, and urban pimps of long ago: caricatures of a bygone era, buried in history.

Section 4

~~~

CONCLUSION

MOVIES ARE A window into America's psyche. Movies that become legendary and classic hit some theme that broils in our subconscious. Love, revenge, and perseverance against tremendous odds are common themes that all great movies possess. But one of the most intriguing themes is the theme of betrayal. In many ways, the Iron Triangle's betrayal of Black America reminds me of the betrayal between brothers Terry Malloy, played by Marlon Brando, and Charley Malloy, played by Rod Steiger, in the 1954 movie masterpiece *On the Waterfront*.

Terry Malloy had been an up-and-coming boxer until his brother persuaded him to start taking dives for a local mob boss. After taking these dives, his life spiraled downward and he becomes a shell of who he once was. His face was scarred. His speech was slurred. His skills were greatly diminished—all while his brother became wealthy and successful in the mob culture. Later Terry decides to retain some of his dignity by testifying against the mob in open court about mob control of the Waterfront. The mob conscripts Terry's brother Charlie to either talk Terry out of testifying or kill him. Terry refused his brother's overtures but during the confrontation with his brother Charlie, Terry, in one of the most iconic scenes in the history of cinema, finally understands it wasn't the mob that destroyed his life. It was his brother, the one who should've looked out for him. Charlie, in an attempt to deflect blame for his brother's downward spiral, said to his brother Terry: "When you were a hundred and sixty-eight pounds you were beautiful. You could have been another Billy Conn. Then that skunk we got you for a manager. He brought you along too fast."

Terry turned to his brother in stunned surprise and said to him:

It wasn't him Charlie. It was you. You remember that night in the garden you came down in my dressing room and said, 'Kid this aint your night. We're going for the price on Wilson.' Remember that? This ain't your night? My night? I could have taken Wilson apart. So what happens? He gets the title shot outdoors in the ball park and what do I get? A one-way ticket to Palookaville. You were my brother, Charlie. You should have looked out for me a little. You should have taken care of me just a little bit so I didn't have to take all them dives for the short-end money."

Charlie said "I had some bets down for you. You saw some money."

Terry said, "You don't understand; I could've had class. I could've been a contender. I could've been somebody, instead of a bum, which is what I am. Let's face it. It was you, Charlie. It was you."

For the past sixty years the Iron Triangle has tried to deflect the cause of all the chaos and all the pain inflicted upon the Black community to elsewhere. Now it's being revealed. It wasn't the White man. It wasn't Republicans. It wasn't America. To the Iron Triangle, consisting of the Black preacher, Black politician, and Black Liberal civic organization leader, I say: "IT WAS YOU!" Every ill in the Black community and most of the ills in America come from this immoral trifecta. IT WAS YOU! It is time to start undoing the damage caused by these very evil people. How do we do that? By attacking them like we attack a disease: identify, isolate, and destroy.

With most diseases, sunlight is the best disinfectant. This book is one of the first rays of sunlight. But with any disease, the people who suffered from the disease the longest are the hardest to cure. There's an old saying "a fool at forty is a fool forever." I do not believe that. The minds of people can be changed. For example: before the 1970s, when a Black person visited a White person's home they had to go to the back door. This was not the law. It was tradition. Black children were taught to do this by their parents and would be punished by their parents if they refused. When young Black people born in the forties came of age in the sixties they refused to submit to the old traditions. They recognized the poverty and disrespect from which Black people suffered came from their willing acceptance of these traditions. They decided to refuse to participate in these traditions and changed the way they were viewed all over the world. Consequently, when the young stopped going to the backdoor the old also stopped going. The young must lead the old again and disavow the old traditions of voting straight Democrat, supporting these civic organizations that double down on failure, and giving tithes and offerings to any preacher that supports a Liberal Democratic Party. You don't have to leave the party. Change it!

I feel sorry for good White Liberals in this environment. It makes sense to believe in the freedom of Black people to really choose their own destiny and to believe that it is condescending and racist to presume to make decisions for adult free people in America—especially a people that has been taught that they were inferior and now you are trying to convince them or agree with them that they are not. If you say they are equal, in your mind, they must be allowed to make their own decisions. However, good White Liberals have taken this to such an extreme that they are willing to watch the Black community commit suicide under the misguided reasoning, "It was their choice." This is the reasoning used by Southern Democrats when asked why the Black slave and the Black sharecropper would not leave the plantation. "It is their choice." That is a cop-out. That is the attitude of a user, not a friend. There is a tradition in this nation that you do not watch another person commit suicide if you can stop it. This is the time for an INTERVENTION. Dr. King said, "Racism is a sickness. These White people are taught that they are better than the Negro." If racism is a sickness, how can the flip side of racism, the feeling that your race is inferior, be any less a sickness? The symptoms of this sickness are evident all over the inner city. The self-destructive behavior and fratricide are indicative of people who hate each other. But we've done nothing to cure that sickness. We've only insisted that White people cure their sickness

When "good" White Liberals look at the problems in these ghettos but then decide to still vote and finance political candidates who have changed nothing in years, they are complicit in every one of the crimes. They are taking advantage of the sickness in the Black community because the Black vote makes their entire Liberal agenda possible.

When the Supreme Court stamped Black people as inferior, with their Brown vs. Board of Education decision, their remedy for our "inferiority" was to forcibly place Black people into closer proximity to the White people who were causing them to feel inferior. It's the equivalent of locking an abused wife in a room with her abusive brute of a husband. Instead of helping Black Americans defeat their inferiority complex they guaranteed that it would continue for generations and their sickness would continue to be exploited.

The Evil White Liberals that control and finance the Iron Triangle led an unsophisticated Black electorate down this primrose path of dependency and despondency. Poor Blacks were offered free health care, free food, free education, housing, and everything they had on the plantation to put these Liberals in power—exploited again by Moscow, the Communists, the Liberal Democrats and the Iron Triangle. It was easy. We all go back to the familiar. The inferior minds (as deemed by the Supreme Court) always look for a master. Even if the master isn't looking for him. Dr. Carter G. Woodson stated that "if you tell a person to go to the back door, go to the back, go to the back door, soon they will go to the back door without being told. If they get there and don't find a back door they, will cut one in." Blacks Americans cut it in and White Liberals provided the saw.

LIBERALS ARE DIVIDING THE CHRISTIANS

Jesus's final prayer before his crucifixion was a prayer for unity. This unity prayer was not only for his disciples and Christians of his day, it was also for us. He knew how Satan was going to come at us. This prayer is recorded in John 17:20:

> My prayer is not for them alone. I pray also for those who will believe in me through their message, that all of them may be one, Father, just as you are in me and I am in you. May they also be in us so that the world may believe that you have sent me, that they may be one as we are one: I in them and you in me. May they be brought to complete unity to let the world know that you sent me and have loved them even as you have loved me.

Because of our disunity, Liberals have taken over our schools, our communities, and our government. They have used race, Confederate monuments, busing, welfare, and gender to make fellow Christians fight and hate one another. None of these things have anything to do with Christianity. Liberals have taken the most powerful country in the history of the world and are using it as a proxy for worldwide abortion, atheism, and LGBTQ activities. Liberals know that if Christians unify there would be no abortion and no violence in our schools. We would have strong families, little poverty, no suicide, and no drug abuse. Liberalism is a death cult that is welcomed in the Democratic Party and every Christian should vacate this party until they are expelled. Have we all forgotten the 2012 Democrat Convention when the Democrats on a voice vote, they voted to leave GOD out of their Party platform? Christians are losing because the left is unified and we Christians are fighting in a burning house. You cannot serve two masters. That now seems to be obvious.

Nevertheless, the Christian Church is reconciling. In 1995 the Southern Baptist Convention, the largest Protestant denomination in America, issued a "Resolution on Racial Reconciliation" on their one hundred fiftieth anniversary. It stated in part:

Whereas, since its founding in 1845, the Southern Baptist Convention has been an effective instrument of God in missions, evangelism and social ministry and

Whereas, The Scriptures teach that Eve is the mother of all living (Genesis 3:20), and that God shows no partiality but in every nation whoever fears him and works righteousness is accepted by him (Acts 10:34-35) and that God has made from one blood every nation of men to dwell on the face on the earth.

Whereas, Our relationship to African Americans has been hindered from the beginning

By the role that slavery played in the formation of the Southern Baptist Convention and

Whereas, Many of our Southern Baptist forebears defended the right to own slaves, and either participated in, supported, or acquiesced in the particularly inhumane nature of American slavery, and

Whereas, in later years Southern Baptists failed, in many cases, to support and in some cases, to support, and in some cases opposed, legitimate initiatives to secure the civil rights of African Americans; and

Whereas, Racism has divided the body of Christ and Southern Baptists in particular, and separated us from our African American brothers and sisters from worship, membership, and leadership and

Whereas, Racism profoundly distorts our understanding of Christian morality, leading some Southern Baptists to believe that racial prejudice and discrimination are compatible with the Gospel and

Whereas, Jesus performed the ministry of reconciliation to restore sinners to a right relationship with the heavenly Father, and to establish right relations among all human beings especially within the family faith.

Therefore, be it RESOLVED, That we, the messengers to the Sesquicentennial meeting of the Southern Baptist Convention, assembled in Atlanta, Georgia, June 20-22, 1995, *unwaveringly denounce racism, in all its forms as deplorable sin . . .*

Be it further RESOLVED, That *we apologize to all African Americans for condoning and/or perpetuating individual and systemic racism in our lifetime, and we genuinely repent of racism of which we have been guilty, whether consciously (Psalm 19:13 or unconsciously (Leviticus 4:27) and*

Be it further RESOLVED, That we ask forgiveness from our African American brothers and sisters, acknowledging that our own healing is at stake: and

Be it further RESOLVED, That we commit ourselves to be doers of the Word (1:22) by pursuing racial reconciliation in all our relationships, especially with our brothers and sisters in Christ (1 John 2:6) to the end that our light would so shine before others that they may see (our) good works and glorify (our) Father in heaven (Matthew 5:16)

Be it finally RESOLVED, That we pledge our commitment to the Great Commission task of making disciples of all people (Matthew 28:19) confessing that in the church of GOD is calling together one people from every tribe and nation (Revelation 5:9), and proclaiming that the Gospel of our Lord Jesus Christ is the only certain and sufficient ground upon which redeemed persons will stand together in restored family union as joint heirs with Christ (Romans 8:17)

My White Christian Conservative brothers and sisters. As I have said before: You have nothing for which to apologize. Do not live in condemnation. Every adult person is responsible for their own lives. Jesus paid for everything. This resolution was passed in 1995. I guess there wasn't any money attached to it because of this writing the Iron Triangle would prefer to reconcile more with the porn industry, hip hop culture, LGBTQ activists, and abortion industry than their fellow brothers and sisters in Christ.

With reconciliation the lucrative "grievance industry" will dry up. The ambulance chasers and stalkers will go bankrupt. Reconciliation has never been the goal of the Iron Triangle. Their goal is conflict, strife, and destruction. Nevertheless, the goal of every Christian must be reconciliation. The opportunity at reconciliation will present itself in thousands of ways but must always be lauded when presented. The world, then, would be saved.

ON THE OTHER HAND

If you happen to not be a Christian or a Patriot, I hope you have the instinct of self-preservation because every accountant is unanimous in agreeing the United States cannot continue borrowing two trillion dollars a year to finance the ills of the ghetto. According to the Cato Institute, federal and state government spent one trillion dollars on social programs in 2014—all of it borrowed. This will continue in perpetuity. Social Security and America will be insolvent in seventeen years if this does not change. So, if you care nothing about the fratricide of the Black race in America? If you care nothing about the unity of all Christians? If you care nothing about your family? If you care nothing about the United States of America? Maybe you care about yourself? Maybe you will understand that the death of Black community is the death of America? Because the death of the Black community will mean that Liberalism has succeeded. It will mean that a cabal of murderers, racists, and atheists now control the most powerful country in the world. They will plunge the world into darkness. They will destroy their host. Look at Detroit and Chicago.

They must destroy. It is their nature.

In explaining how Julius Caesar had taken over Rome, Cassius said to Brutus: "The fault dear, Brutus, is not in our stars, but in ourselves, that we are underlings."

Choose for yourself, but I will not be an underling. I for one will not ask the government for protection or the permission to protect myself. My rights were given to me by GOD, just as my hands and eyes were. Government cannot take away hands and eyes unless I have done something to warrant the confiscation and that is impossible. Likewise the government cannot take away any of my unalienable rights until I first do something to warrant the confiscation and that is impossible. Yet Liberals in government expect citizens to come to them hat in hand asking permission to protect their families, educate their children, practice their religion, and keep the money they've earned. This is how most Black Democrats beg their government. All Black Americans and every other American needs to believe and say with absolution: *"I will no longer ask government or anyone else to guarantee my rights. I defy anyone to try and take them from me."*

C. S. Lewis wrote:

Our Lord finds our desires, not too strong, but too weak. We are half-hearted creatures, fooling about with drink, sex, and ambition when infinite joy is offered us . . . like an ignorant child content to play with mud pies in a slum because he cannot imagine what is meant by the offer of a holiday at the sea. We are far too easily pleased.

If one man demands equality with another man, by making the demand he is in fact admitting he believes he is inferior to the man he is referring to and envious of his status. As heirs of Jesus Christ, we can't be victims and should not be comparing ourselves to anyone. Comparing your life to someone else's life is the very definition of the sins of pride and envy. Pride, the greatest of all sins, leads to hatred, conflict, and strife. The civil rights movement was a movement driven by victimization, envy, and pride. It was devoid of GOD. That is why it failed for Black Americans.

Today the sins of pride, unforgiveness, and envy are front and center in Black America, while guilt and condemnation confounds much of White America. The spirit of pride has convinced Black Democrat Americans that they are right to use the levers of government to force restitution from their fellow Americans for perceived past wrongs some more than one hundred years ago. The refusal of Black Democrats to forgive America, even after six- hundred thousand lives in the Civil War, trillions of dollars in social spending, and thousands of apologies, adds to this toxic mix. Now Black Democratic envy of the "White being," a phantom called White privilege, is an atom bomb. Guilt by a White society suffering from the cancer of condemnation encourages these rabid provocateurs of hate. Nothing can grow here except pain and death. Nothing has grown here except pain and death.

My mother said "when you seek revenge dig two graves." This Liberal way of thinking is absolutely anti-GOD. Jesus demanded forgiveness. He told Peter the denier that he was forgiven, to go forward. He told Paul the murderer that he was forgiven, to go forward. He despised envy and hated pride. He pleaded for us to not live in condemnation. No one can go forward while looking back. If the past sixty years have proven nothing else, the wreckage that is Black America, has proven this metaphor to be absolutely true by now. The Iron Triangle is an entity filled with hate, revenge, and greed. The bucket these Black Democrats seek to fill has no bottom. They never say, "Thank you, America." They only ask for more, more, more. In his "I Have a Dream" speech, Dr. King said, "They ask when will we be satisfied . . . We will not be satisfied until justice rolls down like waters and righteousness like a mighty stream." That is a fancy way of saying "NEVER."

Ask them what amount of money will satisfy them. They can't say. Ask what law needs to be passed. They can't say. Ask them what person needs to be shot. They can't say. They believe there is money in victimization, and they have an open bank account. But this power can be utilized only if the other party agrees to live in condemnation. They never stop demanding, therefore America must stop acquiescing. America must say ENOUGH! This has to end! As long as America gives in to Liberal demands this wound will never heal. These Liberal leeches will take, take, take, and take until the host is dead. I believe that is what they want.

THE WALK OF ILLUMINATION

In 1965 my father took my maternal great-grandfather, Ivie Bond, to the Greyhound Bus Station in Jackson, Tennessee. My great-grandfather was taking a short trip somewhere and my father had gotten him there early. My great-grandfather followed what had been the local custom and went to what had been the colored waiting room and sat down. My father realized that my great-grand father did not know that since he last visited the bus station the 1964 Civil Rights Act had passed and made these separate waiting rooms illegal. My father said to my great-grand father, "Mr. Ivie, you don't have to sit over here anymore. If you like you can go over there where the White folks used to sit." My great-grand father exclaimed surprisingly "sho nuff"? My father said back proudly, "Yes sir." My great-grandfather said, "Well, I'd like to go over there, just to see how the floor walks." He got up, walked over to what had been previously been the "Whites Only" side. He stepped through what had previously been the "Whites Only" doorway. He walked across what had previously been the "Whites Only" floor. He walked back and forth. Stopped. Rocked his feet from side to side. Walked back again and said, "It walks no different."

About the Author

Vince Ellison was born on a cotton plantation in Haywood County, Tennessee.

He studied at Memphis State University (University of Memphis). Vince attained a real-world education while serving five years as a correctional officer at the Kirkland Correctional Institution in Columbia, South Carolina. After resigning his post, Vince began working in the non-profit arena.

In 2000 Vince became the Republican Congressional nominee for the 6th congressional district of South Carolina. Vince has been a conservative columnist, lecturer and frequent guest on many radio and TV talk shows.

He currently resides in the Blue Ridge Mountains of Virginia and the Midlands of South Carolina.

CPSIA information can be obtained
at www.ICGtesting.com
Printed in the USA
LVHW092355270720
661699LV00005B/1203

9 781977 211996